Exploring
Adnams
Country

Exploring
Adnams
Country

PETER THOMAS

Front cover images:
Top: Melford Hall, Long Melford. (NT/Fisheye Images)
Bottom: Bawdsey Estate. (Courtesy of the Bawdsey Manor Estate)

Back cover images:
Top: LT365 *Merbreeze*. (© Lowestoft Maritime Museum)
Middle: The King's Head, Laxfield.
Bottom: The Red Lion, Great Wratting.

First published 2009

The History Press
The Mill, Brimscombe Port
Stroud, Gloucestershire, GL5 2QG
www.thehistorypress.co.uk

© Peter Thomas, 2009

The right of Peter Thomas to be identified as the Author
of this work has been asserted in accordance with the
Copyrights, Designs and Patents Act 1988.

British Library Cataloguing in Publication Data.
A catalogue record for this book is available from the British Library.

ISBN 978 0 7509 5120 3

Printed in Great Britain by Henry Ling Limited, at the Dorset Press,
Dorchester, DT1 1HD

Contents

Foreword

For those of us born and bred in Suffolk many of the scenes and recollections in this book will be familiar. More than that, I think, because there is a feeling of intimacy that comes with discovery. And this book is all about exploring.

The uncovering of many secrets will surprise and, I hope, inspire readers who thought they knew Suffolk. It is pleasing to know that the name and reputation of Adnams has been received so warmly. I liked to hear that the author was welcomed at great country houses during his exploration with the greeting 'We have raised all the blinds, moved the cars and raked the drive for his photographs'.

It is a compliment to the company that the exploration of Suffolk, for that is what the book is, should carry the title 'Adnams Country'. True, the author will have found Adnams pubs and beer wherever he went, but it is the depths of feeling people have for Southwold and the rest of the county that shines through.

Recently we have learned that the lighthouses at Southwold and Lowestoft are not to be closed as navigation beacons for the time being anyway. So much of Suffolk has evidence of its past; there are some fine photographs in the book, especially those in the colour section in the centre.

At the same time Adnams is proud of its innovative record and I am pleased to see a mention of the company's new eco distribution centre we have built at Reydon and the environmental work we have undertaken.

Adnams country is full of profound contrasts such as the Wool Towns, Constable Country and Felixstowe Container Port. More than that, many readers will enjoy their own childhood recollections; blackberry picking, fishing in the river Alde, walking at Shingle Street, or seeing a sailing wherry for the first (perhaps the only) time.

I am pleased to make a modest contribution to the book's publication and wish it every success.

Jonathan Adnams
Executive Chairman
April 2009

Introduction

There can be few country scenes that are so easily recognisable as those painted by John Constable. So familiar are they that the area along the River Stour in south Suffolk became known as Constable Country. He said of them 'They made me a painter'.

Explore the Stour Valley, see it as he did, but do not say 'This is Suffolk'. There is much more than that. Not far downstream from Flatford Mill the river opens out into an estuary; a vision of the *Haywain* is replaced by the sight of a modern continental ferry. The county is one of surprises, of unexpected views: a land waiting to be explored.

No great hills or valleys, never showy or extravagant; it needs to be sought out and wondered at, like the first view of Lavenham Church or the Post Mill at Saxstead. A visit to Shingle Street is a revelation: here is the beauty of solitude.

The purpose of this book is to uncover these secrets, a focus on Southwold, home of the Adnams' family brewery. It is not possible to move far in Suffolk without coming across an Adnams' pub or a free house where Adnams' 'Beer from the coast' is one of the favourite orders.

The only towns of any size in the county are Ipswich, Lowestoft and Bury St Edmunds; otherwise people live in villages and small market towns that occupy the sites of ancient settlements. There are more than 500 medieval country churches in Suffolk and many surviving windmills and watermills, signs of a rural society when wealth came from the land and a former woollen industry. Fortunately the county's slow-moving rivers could not provide enough power for textile factories and there are no coal deposits, so Suffolk was spared the effects of the Industrial Revolution.

Across the gentle countryside the roads of prehistory: innumerable rivers and small streams wind their way towards the North Sea. There, the most easterly coastline in Britain stretches for nearly fifty miles southward from the Waveney Valley to the Stour estuary. Westward, on the Little Ouse River beyond Brandon, Suffolk meets the Fens. On the heathland close to Brandon are the mysterious remains of ancient flint mining, the so-called Grimes Graves. Suffolk people have always been dependent on water; after all, for centuries little ships have set out from sheltered moorings and estuary ports for the fishing grounds or with cargoes of herring, corn, wool, cloth and hides for markets in Europe. The manned lightships that once warned of dangerous sandbanks and shoals have almost disappeared, but some lighthouses remain such as those at Orfordness and Lowestoft. At Southwold the lighthouse stands tall, white and handsome among the houses and the Sole Bay Inn that cluster together on the brink of the low cliffs. Below are the beach huts for which the town is famous; beyond them is the beach, the North Sea and a distant horizon.

A stone's throw from the lighthouse is Adnams' Brewery on East Green; the family whose name it bears have controlled the business ever since they took it over in 1872. Over the years they have created an institution. More than that, the company has been for many Southwold families a way of life. In the local community as a whole, Adnams has always had an important role. In 1990 the Adnams' charity was set up to mark the company's centenary as a public company; the trust fund supports a wide variety of causes 'within 25 miles of the parish church of St Edmund, Southwold'. Of particular interest today is Adnams' support for enterprise education throughout the region; a close long term relationship has been built up with Kirkley High School and Enterprise Lowestoft.

Brewing has been going on in Southwold since 1345 – the longest unbroken tradition of any brewery in England. Although the brewhouse was originally at the Swan Inn, the most important inn in the town, it was moved to the rear of the Swan yard during the re-building after the Great Fire of 1659. The reputation of the Swan's ales grew under successive owners and by the nineteenth century the Sole Bay Brewery had become famous. It passed through a succession of owners until the Adnams brothers arrived from Berkshire in 1872 and took advantage of Southwold's growing popularity for holidays, the fishing and the opening of the Southwold Railway.

Conditions are very different today, but the company flourishes. Innovation continues to be a key theme: evidence of this abounds with the evolution of Cellar and Kitchen Stores, their number being planned to increase to thirty by 2012. Then there is the new award-winning eco-distribution centre and brewery at Reydon: 'A living roof, recycled rainwater and natural cooling'.

Among the many awards Adnams have received, they are particularly proud of bearing the Carbon Trust's Carbon Innovator of the Year distinction; to celebrate this, the first new beer to come out of the Reydon brewhouse was named Adnams' Innovation. The company's award of 'Corporate Social Responsibility' was a further accolade and acknowledges activities such as Adnams' Coastal Cleaning, work carried out by volunteers. Adnams was the first company in the brewing industry to receive the Good Corporation's Ethical Business Award. All this activity that places the company at the forefront of the environmental agenda is headlined by Jonathan Adnams, executive chairman in the phrase 'We believe in doing the right thing'. By any measure business success is being achieved at the same time: in 2007 the Swan Hotel was chosen as Hotel of the Year at the East of England Tourism Awards and the Crown (also at Southwold) was Les Routiers Hotel of the Year, Central and Eastern England.

Now a recognised and successful advertising slogan 'Beer from the Coast' used with illustrations on beer mats and postcards is a reminder of Adnams' major product and the basis of the company's growing prosperity. Among the well known labels, Adnams' Bitter, already an award-winning beer, was CAMRA's Champion Beer of East Anglia in 2007. Traditional beer at its best, it is the brewery's pride and joy. Broadside is its excellent companion and was originally brewed to celebrate the tercentenary of the Battle of Sole Bay. Such is the confidence in the

Behind the Swan Hotel, on East Green, is Adnams' Sole Bay Brewery. Nearby, in Victoria Street, is one of their Cellar and Kitchen stores.

The famous Sole Bay Inn and the lighthouse are only a step or two from the brewery.

future that an ambitious strategic plan has been adopted in which it is aimed to double the company's profits over a five year period. Jonathan Adnams believes that the aim can be achieved by building on the strength of the Adnams' brand and a commitment to doing the right thing.

History has shown time and again that rivers are more than exits to a wider world; they are also highways to the interior. None more so than those of Suffolk, with plenty of safe anchorages in the estuaries and many possible routes into the fertile country inland. This was always a vulnerable, even an inviting coast for raiders and invaders; in the Dark Ages with the Roman Forts on the Saxon Shore abandoned and unmanned there was little lasting peace. Little hope either, for there was neither unity here, nor any organised defence. Almost at will, the Anglo-Saxons swept over the country, destroying what they did not want, taking what they did, and settling where they liked. Indeed, bringing a new population to this part of the country.

No surprise then, that in the course of time a regional identity established itself: East Anglian. Its separateness was deep: even today in the local dialect, place names, culture and the general way of life, the people of Suffolk cling to their prized Anglo-Saxon heritage, their wish to 'do different'. Just to confuse the rest of the world, consider the ordinary word 'do', pronounced locally 'dew' and its variety of uses. As an order it could be 'Dew you go and git some taters from the garden', or as a warning in a shop window 'Bring your repair ticket with you dew you can't hev your shoes', or to describe a strange happening 'Thass'a rum owd dew'.

Life was hard over the centuries: clearing woodland, hedging, ditching, ploughing and harvesting the fields. The seasons determined the work to be done and the time for it; the pace of life depended more on the calendar than the clock and coloured attitudes, even producing a local sense of humour. I like the reply of the porter at the village railway station when asked by a departing passenger 'What time is the next train?' 'Thass' jus gone, I'm afraid'.

Perhaps too the landscape's gentle contours, the lack of real hills or anything dramatic other than the majestic skies strengthens the feeling of permanence and acceptance of the world as it is. Ever since the Anglo-Saxons came as settlers and created small communities, these have grown gradually, mainly from nearby. Even that was cautious; if you were born on the Suffolk side of the River Waveney, the accepted wisdom used to be to take care if you thought of marrying someone from the Norfolk side.

If any test of the beauty of this countryside were needed, it would be met by recognising the number of painters who were born, settled, or visited Suffolk. Apart from John Constable, Thomas Gainsborough was born at Sudbury; his house and gallery can be visited. Alfred Munnings was born at Mendham in Suffolk and settled at Dedham, just across the Stour from East Bergholt, Constable's birthplace. Walberswick, on the opposite side of the River Blyth from Southwold attracted painters for many years: the Newberys from the Glasgow art world came with Philip Wilson Steer, followed by Charles Rennie Mackintosh in 1914. The Mackintosh watercolours of countryside flowers such as broom and fritillary, as well as garden plants, are remarkable.

Inspiration was not confined to painters: Benjamin Britten was born at Lowestoft and settled at Aldeburgh. His work such as *Peter Grimes* captured the atmosphere of the coastline and its people; he and his friend Peter Pears were responsible for creating the Aldeburgh Music Festival. Their memorial is a fine concert hall at Snape Maltings, just a few miles upstream from Aldeburgh on the River Alde.

Then there were the nineteenth-century writers: George Crabbe, whose work included *The Borough* from which the story of *Peter Grimes* comes and Edward Fitzgerald, probably best known for his translation of the *Rubaiyat of Omar Khayyam* in 1859.

And what a coastline this is! From Lowestoft, Oulton Broad and the River Waveney in the north, Southwold, Dunwich, Minsmere RSPB, Sizewell Nuclear Power Station, Snape Maltings, Orfordness, Woodbridge and Sutton Hoo on the Deben, Shingle Street to Felixstowe, the River Orwell and Ipswich.

It is some fifty miles from the coast at Southwold or Lowestoft to Newmarket and the county border with Cambridgeshire. The chalky down-like hills of the horse gallops are a far cry from the sandy heathlands inland between Southwold and Blythburgh, Woodbridge and Orford. Large areas of conifers have been planted to form forests such as that at Rendlesham; they flourish in the light soil of what is known as the Sandlings.

West of the A12 Ipswich-Lowestoft Road is a plateau of boulder clay left by the glaciers and well suited to growing cereals, particularly barley for brewing and for sugar beet; the huge expanses of yellow in summer tell of the increasing acreage of oilseed rape. The claylands and the chalk area even further west are the source of flints which has been traditionally used in church building, especially for the characteristic Suffolk decoration called flushwork. Beyond the clay and chalk areas north of Bury St Edmunds is a second region of wind-blown sands and heaths called Breckland that merges into Norfolk near Thetford.

Another dividing line in Suffolk is the A14 from Bury to Ipswich, sometimes called the Lark/Gipping 'corridor' from the river system there. South of that line the rolling countryside and the rivers that powered the early textile industry merge into Essex; people visualise London as close enough for this to be almost commuter country. North of the A14 the landscape becomes increasingly remote; it is arable country where farming is the mainstay of the economy, where boys used always to say that they would leave school, not in the summer, but 'at harvest'. Pantile roofs are the rule, not the exception and there are more round tower churches the further north you go.

With a scattered population and a lack of large towns there was not likely to be a bright future for Suffolk's rural railways. Sure enough, even the northern section of the East Suffolk line from Beccles to Yarmouth Southtown fell victim to the axe; the story of the Suffolk branch lines is told elsewhere in the following pages. For railway lovers a visit to the museum at Brockford station near Wetheringsett will bring on a heavy attack of nostalgia. The station houses a section of the Mid-Suffolk Light Railway; work started on its building from a junction at Haughley near Stowmarket, but the line never reached its destination – Halesworth.

It was always said that 'all roads lead to Bury St Edmunds'. Many in the past who went that way were, no doubt, pilgrims visiting the shrine of Edmund King and Martyr; because of the abbey built at this shrine and of the cathedral, the town is really the spiritual capital of Suffolk.

Breckland at Knettishall Heath, a country park near the Norfolk border.

This book gives it special attention, the nearby countryside with contrasting attractions such as Ickworth House, a jewel in The National Trust's crown and the West Stow Anglo-Saxon Village. Lavenham and Long Melford, the wonderfully preserved 'wool towns' are not far away and Stowmarket has a fine collection and displays at its Museum of East Anglian Life.

The north of the county has its contrasts too: within a strange loop of the River Waveney reluctant to reach the sea is Lothingland near Lowestoft, where the Danes settled. Near Oulton Broad is the extravagant Somerleyton Hall, built by Sir Morton Peto, who bought the estate in 1844. Close by is Fritton Lake, some two miles long, formed like the Norfolk Broads by ancient peat cutting, or turbary; it was once used as a decoy for trapping wildfowl.

The Waveney's course upstream takes increasing numbers of leisure craft to Beccles. Further still near Diss is a monument in a field at Hoxne marking the place where King Edmund was murdered by Danish invaders; the source of the river is in a marsh near Redgrave.

Oddly, only a few yards away in the same marsh is the source of the Little Ouse that flows west, leaving the Waveney and Suffolk behind.

No visitor to this north western part of Suffolk should miss the palatial Euston Hall, home of the Duke and Duchess of Grafton; their collection of paintings of the Court of King Charles II is unique. Across the A11 that seems to separate Breckland from the rest of the county are Lakenheath and Mildenhall, well known for their air bases; both have outstanding churches. That at Mildenhall, dedicated to St Mary and St Andrew, has one of the most memorable east windows dated 1300. Its timbered roof is breathtaking with its carving; the tie beams of the nave are brilliantly decorated with angels carrying scrolls.

This book aims to highlight some of the outstanding features that an exploration of Adnams Country offers. Not all, by any means, because of the limitations of space that make choices necessary. History does not stand still and new ideas may cry out for recognition: the Felixstowe Container Terminal was built and expands, a new tower was completed for Bury Cathedral and China has returned to Lowestoft.

In ancient times Suffolk was known as '*selig*', since corrupted into 'silly'. Selig's original meaning was 'holy' or 'blessed' and so it will always be.

Towns

Southwold

Any exploration of Adnams Country should begin at Southwold. The town, according to Pevsner is 'One of the happiest and most picturesque seaside towns in England'; the town's guide says that it has a 'unique quietude'. Certainly it is a modest town; its buildings do not compete for attention and its development has been in the best of good taste. If you are looking for fairgrounds, don't go to Southwold, but the shops on the High Street are a delight; be prepared for leisurely shopping as it is a social event, with people meeting others they know and having news to pass on. Thursday is an especially busy day when local growers and traders open their market stalls round the Town Pump on the Market Place. Looking down on their activity is the Swan Hotel, Adnams' flagship, not only a haven for those in town and looking for refreshment in comfort, but also in great demand for quality holidays. With a history going back to the seventeenth century, the Swan has been extended – tastefully upwards and eastwards, the last extension being in 1938.

Only a few steps past the neighbouring Town Hall, East Street leads beyond Adnams' Lord Nelson pub to the Sailors' Reading Room (open to the public) on the cliff edge with the famous beach huts and sea below. Northwards, the Promenade and North Parade attract many visitors to the Pier, where the car park is free in the winter, but en route is the great white lighthouse. Surrounded by red-roofed houses and the Adnams' Sole Bay Inn, the pub is one of the many reminders of the battle that took place between a combined British and French fleet and the Dutch on 28 May 1672. It was inconclusive, although the Earl of Sandwich was killed when the Royal James was sunk. James, Duke of York used Sutherland House at the western end of the High Street as his headquarters; it dates from the sixteenth century and has handsome decorated plaster ceilings. A plaque on the front wall commemorates its history.

Oddly enough, Sole Bay no longer exists, as scouring by the sea swept away the headlands that once enclosed it. (see Dunwich p. 116)

The Southwold colourful town sign shows men of war at sea under full sail, but the enduring image of the town is surely its magnificent parish church of St Edmund, martyred King of East Anglia. The stained glass of the east window includes his martyrdom at the hands of the invading Danes. That story is told elsewhere in this book. Like so many churches in the area, St Edmunds was constructed of flint with stone dressings. The 100ft tower is a fine example of flushwork decoration for which flint is famous. The south porch is also beautifully decorated with flushwork in a chequerboard pattern and dark flint initials at its foot. The eighteen clerestory windows along the nave give the church a majestic feel that is repeated inside where the high timbered roof has alternate hammer beams and arched braces. The extraordinary rood screen extends across the nave and aisles; gilded and colourful, the lower panels are painted with thirty-six figures of apostles and angels. The decorated hour-glass pulpit and the carvings on the arms of the choir stalls are superb and there is, of course, the Clock Jack, close to the tower arch, rung at the start of services.

Although fire destroyed an earlier church in 1430, today's St Edmunds, completed in 1460, survived the Great Fire of 1659, which left only the church and Sutherland House standing in Southwold. In all, 238 houses were lost; the rebuilding of Southwold was carried out around nine Greens which made an effective fire break, or so it is said. The result has been small neighbourhoods of Georgian, Regency and Victorian houses in groups round spacious grass lawns.

As at Southwold, beach huts are popular and the town remains a destination for family holidays.

Gun Hill is one of the attractive 'Greens' planned after a great fire and boasts the town's defences.

The settings attracted wealthy residents; even the smaller houses and cottages became much in demand, creating a resort town of great character.

South Green, just off the High Street is a good example; beyond it is Gun Hill with its surprising battery of six 18-pounder culverins presented to Southwold during the reign of George II to defend the town. They are said to have been given by the Duke of Cumberland after his victory over the Scots at Culloden in 1746, but another theory is that they were presented to Southwold Corporation by the Board of Ordnance.

From South Green and Gun Hill, Ferry Road leads south along the line of the seashore to the Lifeboat Station and the harbour mouth. The Southwold bank of the Blyth is known as Blackshore, the home of the Sailing Club and the moorings of the fishermen… If your love is fresh fish, this is where to go; notices on the shed tell you what is on offer and the prices.

There is a pedestrian ferry there in summer across to Walberswick, and if you walk to the end of the unsurfaced road you can sample Adnams' Harbour Inn. In the desperate days of the 1953 East Coast floods people were marooned there; the height of the flood is marked on the wall.

The Bailey Bridge for pedestrians is close by; either cross the river to Walberswick, or follow the former railway track to Southwold. From the Harbour Inn, York Road leads back to the town past the Water Tower; this route is a boon to explorers of Adnams Country whose mobility is limited and who rely on their cars. On the left is the Golf Club and the Common; presented to the town as an open space in 1509.

In spite of the Battle of Sole Bay and Dutch rivalry over North Sea fisheries, peaceful relations with the Dutch grew – remember their efficiency in draining the Fens – and their influence was seen increasingly in Southwold and Suffolk. Do not miss Church Street in Southwold, an inconspicuous turning between the shops on High street not far from the Swan Hotel.

The left-hand side of Church Street is lined with brick-built, white or colourwashed cottages. Pantiled roofs, uniform fronts and varied dormers are strongly Dutch in style. At the end of the street a left turn leads to Bartholomew Green and the church; to the right is East Green and Adnams' Brewery.

Adnams' pubs:

Swan Hotel	Market Place, Southwold	01502 722186 (Accomm)
Red Lion	South Green, Southwold	01502 722385
Sole Bay Inn	East Green, Southwold	01502 723736
Lord Nelson Inn	East Street, Southwold	01502 722079
Kings Head	High Street, Southwold	01502 724517 (Accomm)
Harbour Inn	Blackshore, Southwold	01502 722381
Blyth Hotel	Station Road, Southwold	01502 722632 (Accomm)
Randolph Hotel	41 Wangford Road, Reyford	01502 723603 (Accomm)

Bury St Edmunds

There will be some readers of this book who can remember when Bury St Edmunds was the County Town of West Suffolk – but no longer. The 1974 reorganisation of local government, creating Suffolk a single county and Ipswich its County Town, brought to an end 1,000 years

The classic view of Southwold, with Adnams' Swan Hotel looking over the market on a busy day.

of Bury's role as a spiritual and administrative capital of a huge territory originally known as the Liberty of St Edmund.

The dominance of Bury St Edmunds began after the martyrdom of Edmund in 870 at the hands of the Danish invaders and his burial at a shrine at Beodricsworth, as the town was known in 903. A chapel was built at the shrine, attracting many pilgrims and cared for by monks. The coming of the Normans and the building of a great abbey at Bury ensured the continued importance of St Edmundsbury as the town came to be called. At the Dissolution of the Monasteries in 1539, the Liberty of St Edmund reverted to the Crown; responsibility for the area passed to West Suffolk County Council in 1889. So much for Bury's history; no other part of Suffolk compares with the town for opportunities for exploration. Some 1,000 buildings have been listed as being of architectural and historic importance. The town's layout to the west of the abbey was planned by the abbots; a grid pattern that was unique then. Abbeygate Street and Angel Hill are a fascinating introduction to the abbey ruins; pedestrians pass through the Great Gate into the Abbey Gardens that slope down to the River Lark and the Abbot's Bridge. Built about 1090, the abbey was longer than Norwich Cathedral; it was said that 'the highest points of Christendom' were St Peter's, Rome, Cologne Cathedral and Bury Abbey Church. The west front of the church exists today with a number of houses built into it. Of the rest of the abbey, the crossing piers still stand, together with the north wall of the transept – enough to show the enormous size of the building. The outline of the crypt can be seen; this is where the shrine of St Edmund once stood. Its destruction, the story of the disappearance of the saint's remains and of the Bury St Edmunds cross follows this chapter.

Do not leave the abbey ruins without looking at the plaque on one of the piers of the crossing tower. It records the date of St Edmund's martyrdom and a pilgrimage made here by the barons of England in 1214 to swear a solemn oath to force King John to sign a charter granting all men their true liberty. The following year the King signed the Magna Carta at Runnymede: Bury became known as 'Shrine of a King, Cradle of the Law'.

The St Edmundsbury Cathedral was St James Parish Church until 1913. Its Millennium Tower was completed in 2000.

The west front of the abbey church
has several newer houses built into it.

Edmund, king and martyr, is
remembered as a young man close to
the abbey church's west front.

The little chapel of St Stephen at Bures near Sudbury, where Edmund was crowned at the age of fifteen.

Across the front of the abbey precinct is the lovely square: Angel Hill, where medieval fairs were held. Today there are Georgian-fronted houses, the ivy-clad Angel Hotel made famous by Charles Dickens and, on the south side, the Athenaeum with its glorious ballroom by Robert Adam. Between the abbey west front and the cathedral is a poignant statue of Edmund.

We know that he was crowned king at Bures near Sudbury on Christmas Day 855; it was then a capital of East Anglia. Just north of the village a simple thatched chapel stands on a hill where traditionally the coronation took place. Go up Cuckoo Hill as far as the farm buildings on the right, then take a public footpath across fields to the Chapel of St Stephen. It is worth asking for the keys at the neighbouring house; the original dedication cross is still visible inside the door. Remarkably there are also tombs of the de Veres, Earls of Oxford, removed from Earls Colne Priory in Essex at the Suppression of the Monasteries.

Bury's prosperity continued in medieval times through the marketing of cloth produced there and at the famous Wool Towns of the Stour Valley. The wealth of the clothiers was responsible for the rebuilding of many parish churches; Bury was no exception with its Churches of St James and St Mary, the former becoming the cathedral of the Diocese of St Edmundsbury and Ipswich in 1913.

The elevation of St James' Church to the status of a cathedral was followed by a number of extensions, the most recent being the eagerly awaited Millennium Tower completed in 2005 in the Gothic style and clad in stone from Barnack near Stamford. Previously the nearby Norman tower, gateway to the great west door of the abbey church served the purpose and housed the bells of St James. The new quire successfully linked modern work with the St James' medieval craftsmanship. The style of painting between the hammer beams of the nave was repeated in the quire which contains the Bishop's Throne. The carving includes a wolf guarding the head of St Edmund, part of the traditional account of his murder. (see Hoxne, p. 138).

The cathedral has a remarkable collection of 1,000 kneelers worked in every parish of the diocese and bearing a symbol of each. Visitors take great pride in finding the kneeler from their own parish.

In 1465 the abbey church was destroyed by fire. Perhaps St Edmund's shrine and his remains were lost then; the inventory completed at the Dissolution of the Monasteries made no mention of the coffin, giving rise to much speculation. Had the coffin already been removed for safe keeping, had it been lost, or even had the relics been taken to an abbey at Toulouse as some documents suggest? We shall never know the truth.

The Bury St Edmunds Cross

The sudden appearance of the Cross at Zurich after the end of the Second World War is another mystery. Dating From 1180 it is some 22in high and is made of walrus tusk; Latin inscriptions on it coincide with wording on manuscripts from the Bury Abbey Library. Probably it survived the Dissolution in 1539 by being taken to a mother church in France. Exactly how the cross came into the possession of the dealer will never be known, but we can surmise that it was looted during the Occupation of France then passed as a spoil of war to an allied serviceman. The dealer stated that he had bought it on that basis; its legal ownership was always in doubt, although it was confirmed as an authentic relic. It was eventually bought by the Metropolitan Museum in New York, where it is on display in the cloisters. A figure of the crucified Christ that was originally attached to it came to light later and was replaced. It is truly astonishing and needs to be seen by anyone who has been to the Abbey of St Edmundsbury.

St Mary's Church

Do not overlook this lovely building; it is only a stone's throw from the Cathedral and was longer than St James prior to the extensions there. The nave roof is superb, with alternate hammer beams and arch braces decorated with figures of saints and angels in abundance. A north porch from the mid-fifteenth century with fan vaulting was paid for by John Nottyngham, a local grocer. John Baret's tomb of 1467 is decorated with shields and was placed in the south aisle under a panelled roof which shows the motto 'Grace me governe'. More surprising is the tomb in the chancel of a former Queen of France, Mary Tudor, sister of King Henry VIII, first married to Louis XII of France and then widowed. Her second husband was Charles Brandon,

St Edmund's Church, Southwold, has many attractive features, not least the east window showing the martyred king.

The mysterious cross of St Edmund is on display at
the Cloisters Museum in New York.

Duke of Suffolk. She was buried at the Abbey, but Henry VIII, anxious about the consequences
of the Dissolution, ordered that she be reburied in St Mary's.

The Theatre Royal

Only a few steps from St Mary's along Crown Street to its junction with Westgate Street is
the finest surviving Regency theatre in England, built by William Wilkins in 1819. It has had a
major restoration programme with a planned reopening in September 2007; in the care of The
National Trust, it has a regular programme of drama, music, comedy and dance. Its beautiful
and intimate auditorium, decorated 'sky' ceiling and many original features make the Theatre
Royal a visit not to miss when exploring Bury St Edmunds; guided tours can be booked. Call
the theatre on 01284 769505 for opening times and prices.

Moyses Hall

Now a museum housing items of local interest, it was once a dwelling house dating from 1180
and is a landmark in the Market Place. Almost opposite is the Market Cross of 1774 built by
Robert Adam: this was originally the Town Hall and once had a market on the ground floor.

The old Guildhall, Corn Exchange and Unitarian Chapel should be on any explorer's list
too; of endless pleasure and interest are the attractive shop fronts, especially in Abbeygate Street
leading down to Angel Hill, opposite the Abbey Gate. Allow plenty of time to explore Bury
St Edmunds: Alec Clifton-Taylor's book *Bury St Edmunds* closes by saying 'A day would hardly
suffice to relish all the good things which this town still has to offer'.

Any visitor to Bury St Edmunds should know of Adnams' Red Lion at Great Wratting, just
off the A143 to Bury, a few miles north of Haverhill. (Look for B1061 Kedington crossroads). It
is unusual – excellent too – framing the door is a massive arch of whalebone that has stood there
throughout living memory. At one time a lamp was fitted to it, perhaps to light the entrance. It
was a popular custom in the nineteenth century to use whalebone for decorative purposes and
it is likely that a former landlord of the Red Lion was a mariner – probably a whaler. Of the

The Theatre Royal. (© Martin Rushworth/Theatre Royal, Bury)

The newly restored interior of the Theatre Royal. (© Martin Rushworth./Theatre Royal, Bury)

hundreds of whalebone arches that once existed around the country only eighty or so are left today. The famous one on the West Cliff at Whitby was set up as a monument to the men of the whaling industry; others were made from the remains of wounded or beached animals. Most are to be found along the coasts of the Western Isles or the north east coast of England. Lincolnshire has one at Threekingham between Grantham and Boston, not a great distance from the east coast, commemorating a nineteenth-century whaling expedition by the local Cragg family.

Another unusual feature of the Red Lion is the huge collection of brassware. Don't try to count, just admire it and the energy of the landlady and her staff: they spend half an hour each day cleaning and polishing it. It takes two months to clean it all, then they start all over again, just like painting the Forth Bridge! To be in the company of local regulars for lunch is always a good sign and that is what you will find at the Red Lion.

Adnams' pub:

Red Lion   School Road, Great Wratting   01440 783237

Lowestoft: The Scores and the Beach Village

The Scores, or passageways, are characteristic of 'Old' Lowestoft; in some ways they are similar to the Rows at Great Yarmouth, but because Lowestoft was first built along the cliff edge, the Scores go steeply down to the foreshore called the Denes. At Gunton, just north of Lowestoft, the foreshore has the name Dunes, so Denes is probably a derivation from this.

The curious name 'score' is believed to derive from 'to scow', as some were natural formations scoured into the cliffs; others were developed by current usage. On the Denes below the High Street houses were workplaces serving the fishing industry, such as net stores and fish curing sheds, so there was regular use of the Scores. Steps, handrails and walls were built on them and the surfaces were eventually paved; the names of the Scores changed over the years, although Lighthouse Score at the north end of the Denes has retained its name. The present lighthouse was opened for use in 1874; its high position and great power means that it can be seen seventeen miles out to sea. It is now automated and is no longer manned.

Further south along High Street, or on Whapload Road below, is Mariner's Score, which has a pointed arch at the High Street end and giving a good view through it of the foreshore and the sea. There was once a Mariner's Inn, from which the name comes, although it was originally called Swan Score because of the Swan Inn that stood at the top end. Today the Town Hall faces across the High Street there. At the bottom there was once a second navigation beacon, the Lowestoft Low Light; ships at sea were able to navigate the sandbanks offshore by lining up that light with the main lighthouse. Trinity House was responsible for both of these lights as far back as 1609, making the Suffolk coast the first to have a planned maritime lighting system.

Visiting the Scores can be a strenuous walk, but if you plan it carefully and remember that for every 'up' there is a 'down' you will enjoy the Scores Trail enormously.

The old houses on the High Street are well worth looking for, there is also an historic pub, the Crown, one of the oldest in the town at the top of Crown Score to pause for refreshment (there are forty-eight steps on that Score!). The walls along Crown Score are typical brick and pebble (flint) and curious sculpted crabs are set at the base of the walls.

The Beach Village

If any part of Lowestoft could represent the town's lost herring fishery and the way of life that went with it, this was it. The 'Beach', or the 'Grit' as the locals used to call it has gone following the clearance of the 1960s, but the Scores that led down to the Village are still there. The name for the Beach Village 'Town below the Cliff' concealed the appalling conditions there, poor housing, few basic facilities, large families and low pay; sometimes no pay at all after a week or more at sea if there was no catch. During times of depression there was little to be done to support a family, except perhaps beachcombing for coal or wood. No wonder they were called 'Gritsters'.

Somehow businesses made a living: bakers and butchers, for example, and there were thirteen pubs. The last closed in the 1960s: the Gas House Tavern in 1966 and the Rising Sun (known as the Japanese Embassy) the very last, in 1968.

By 1863 there was a Primitive Methodist Chapel and in February the Beach Village had its own parish church, Christ Church. The chapel was demolished, but Christ Church on Whapload Road remains, although the crowded back streets of the Village it served have been replaced by the Birds Eye factory buildings.

Along the foreshore stood curing houses, warehouses and fishermen's sheds (or 'shods') used for their gear and for social purposes as well. In view of conditions in the village it is no surprise that smuggling was not uncommon. Nevertheless the beachmen served on the lifeboat; the first was set up in 1801. The long-serving and well-known coxswains of the lifeboat service were from the village and were recognised with their crews for saving many lives.

Most of the beachmen went fishing, but a few were employed at the Eagle Brewery, at the salt factory near Ness Point, or at the Rope Works, but it was the herring season that gave the village a chance to survive. The Scottish fishergirls took lodgings as near as possible to their 'Pickling Plots' and close to Hamilton Dock where the drifters landed their catch. There, the girls gutted and packed the fish, layering them with salt, such were the quantities of fish they handled (in all weathers) that the plots were covered with line after line of stacked barrels. Carts were lined up waiting to move the catch to trains or to load on to ships serving the market for Russia.

It is only old photographs that can tell you the real story of the Beach Village. There had been a depression in fishing in the 1930s and serious damage was done in the village by bombing in the Second World War, followed by an undermining of the sea wall which threatened the village by flooding in 1946. This was averted, but in 1953 there were the worst floods ever experienced on the east coast. These caused irreparable damage; people left the area, a new sea wall was completed, but there seemed to be no future for the village. The council decided to clear the area and to rehouse those remaining. The demolitions resulted in the disappearance of the Beach Village.

But a visit to Lowestoft is not complete without a visit to the area where 2,500 people lived and worked. Along Whapload Road are still buildings from the Beach Village days and the net drying area, at the north end there is Sparrow's Nest, the attractive park by the lighthouse once owned by the Sparrow family and bought by the corporation in 1897. Below, on the Denes, a sports ground, the Denes Oval, was laid out.

See, too, the most easterly point in the UK: Ness Point and the unusual geoscope, laid out in coloured stone marking points of the compass and showing directions and distances to places like the Dogger Bank and the Gas Fields. It points to the direction of the summer solstice and to Edinburgh which it says is just 516 miles away.

Standing at the north end of Whapload Road is the Lowestoft Maritime Museum, just below Sparrow Nest Park and the lighthouse. The volunteer museum attendants are ex-seamen and others interested in the port of Lowestoft.

Since its establishment in 1968 the museum has been extended twice and specialises in the history of the Lowestoft fishing fleet. Hundreds of items are on display that illustrate trawling and the earlier system of drift-net fishing. A full scale replica of the aft cabin of a drifter shows how crews lived on board and there is an extensive collection of shipwrights' tools. Pictures show how the fishing fleet developed from sailing 'smacks' to steam drifters and modern diesel trawlers. Part of the collection illustrates Lowestoft's wartime association with the Royal Navy and there is a fine exhibition of the history of lifeboats. The museum is open daily from May to October and will open specially out of season for parties of eight or more. Call 01502 561963 for further information. There is a free car park nearby.

Opening Times:

Daily May to October
Out of season for parties of eight or more
Tel: 01502 561963

Directions:

A12 northbound traffic should cross the bridge and turn right into Waveney Road and Battery
Green Road
At large roundabout leading into Old Nelson Street keep right into Whapload Road
A12 southbound traffic should keep left at St Peter's Street roundabout into Old Nelson Street
At the Battery Green roundabout turn left into Whapload Road

Lowestoft: From Fishing Village to Health Resort

Lowestoft's 'centre of gravity' seems to have moved over the centuries. Why, otherwise, is the
parish church of St Margaret's so far out of town and the Town Hall a substantial and strenuous
walk up the High Street away from the bus station and the shopping centre?

As a village community 1,000 years ago life must have depended as much on the land as on
the sea, when both farming and fishing supported life. No surprise then, that St Margaret's was
located to serve the original agricultural village. The increasing importance of the herring fishery to Lowestoft led to a movement of population closer to the seashore; fisher folk themselves
were eventually to settle at the foot of the cliffs, while on the cliff top along the present High
Street were the larger homes of merchants and smokehouse owners.

It was a gradual change – as Lowestoft grew there was a westward move, even later, southward, too, across the river. The fishing industry, also general cargo handling, had to operate off
the beach before the town had a harbour, so the Denes along the seashore became a hive of
activity. Times were hard and many lives were lost at sea. It took Lowestoft many years and
much effort to achieve its Royal Charter of Incorporation and the borough to have its first
mayor. The Town Hall was built in 1857; in 1900 it had to be rebuilt further back to allow for
road widening, but events had already moved on at the other end of town. A harbour had
been built and by 1834 river traffic was passing through the New Cut to and from Norwich,
avoiding restrictions placed on cargoes through Great Yarmouth. There was much animosity
between the two towns over business controls.

Lowestoft harbour, the bridge and the town's railway connection focused business further south.
Shops on the High Street lost business to bigger stores on what is now the pedestrianised shopping
area, London Road North. The Triangle, once a large and well-loved market site at the end of the
High Street began to decline too, leaving the Town Hall in some isolation.

Today's traffic on the High Street in north Lowestoft is limited to that going south because
it is so narrow. Most of the shops are small and provide 'convenience' service. Large buildings such as the Town Hall and the Crown Hotel are notably different, although there is still
evidence of the houses of the wealthy along the cliff edge. No. 55 is one of these, dating from
about 1770 and built in red brick; it has an attractive columned doorway with a segmental
arch and rich decoration.

An interesting historic point close by is at the corner of High Street and Martin's Score, a
few steps south of the Crown Hotel. A plaque with an illustration of a ship in full sail is headed
'The Armada Post' and stands above an unimpressive post said to have been originally erected
in 1688, exactly 100 years after the defeat of the Spanish Armada. The post has the initials TM,
said to be those of Thomas Meldwn of Lowestoft, whose ship *Elizabeth* took part in the battle.
The post has been replaced successively in 1788, 1888 and 1988.

Lowestoft's South Beach and Promenade, looking towards the pier and Yacht Club.

Benjamin Britten's name has been given to the shopping centre connecting the pedestrianised London Road North with the bus station, road traffic going north in Lowestoft has to pass along Battery Green Road on the east, or Katwijk Way on the west. They come together at the junction of the A12 and the A1144 leading to Oulton Broad, where there are massive peak-hour delays at the Oulton Broad North railway crossing. There are two rail routes out of Lowestoft today; one is the easternmost section of the East Suffolk line which has one stop at Oulton Broad South before reaching Beccles and destinations to Ipswich and Liverpool Street. The other route leads to Norwich and stops at Oulton Broad North, Somerleyton, Reedham and various stations across the marshes of the Waveney and the Yare to reach the city.

For the development of Lowestoft south of the river, see the Peto Story (p. 25). The South and Claremont Piers were built respectively in 1846 and 1903, allowing Londoners to arrive by sea.

The establishment of the Royal Norfolk and Suffolk Yacht Club and Basin alongside the South Pier brought a wider clientele to the town, raising its prestige and matching the large, comfortable hotels that had opened to the south of Lowestoft. Children's Corner and sands near the South Pier became very popular for sea bathing, and chalets were built along the sea front southwards. A boating lake and open spaces such as Kensington Gardens and Normanston Park as well as Sparrows Nest and Nicholas Everitt's Park at Oulton Broad all helped attract visitors. Sports events were catered for on the Denes Oval.

A tram service, converted into buses in the 1930s served the widening district once Pakefield and Oulton Broad were incorporated with Lowestoft itself.

Two of the town's most illustrious sons were Benjamin Britten, born on Kirkley Cliff Road and George Davison, famous in nineteenth-century photography who was born on Marine Parade. Writers who visited or stayed included Charles Dickens (remember *Blundeston* and *David Copperfield*), George Borrow and Joseph Conrad who arrived through Lowestoft Harbour.

None of these, including Benjamin Britten would recognise much of Lowestoft today after so much change. Fishing is all but gone, together with its support industries such as net and ice making, herring curing and ship building; lost also has been Eastern Coachworks and Pye TV manufacturing. But on the site of the old Beach Village is an industrial estate with the giant Birds Eye frozen-food plant occupying much of the space. Huge on the skyline are the oil rigs being built for the North Sea Field; services for established rigs have become an essential industry to help replace the lost fisheries. But Lowestoft's continued prosperity also depends on its success as a health resort. Visit the East Point Pavilion and see evidence of the town's confidence in the future.

Lowestoft: The Peto Story

Denmark Road in Lowestoft runs westward from the railway station, becoming Peto Way, passing Leathes Ham, on to Normanston Drive, then reaches Oulton Broad.

There's Rotterdam Road too; I once thought they were Lowestoft's reminders of Danish invaders and Dutch trading connections. Now, knowing better, I realise that Denmark Road commemorates not warlike Danes, but the 'North of Europe Steam Navigation Service' set up by Samuel Morton Peto as a means of importing cattle from Denmark for sale at Smithfield Market. It was an enterprising idea to expand the use of Lowestoft harbour (which he owned) and provide traffic for the railway (which he had promoted) even if the shipping line was not a long-term solution.

Peto was one of those Victorian businessmen whose horizons were limitless; on the death of his uncle he joined Thomas Grissell as a partner in the family's London building business in 1830 and was quickly involved with Charles Barry's work in Trafalgar Square. Later he won the contract for work on the Houses of Parliament, when he joined forces with John Thomas, a sculptor. Thomas continued working as Peto's designer for the Lowestoft development that became one of his many projects.

Once Peto had entered the profitable, but risky, business of railway building he accumulated untold wealth; it is said that he was involved in contracts for a seventh of the wildly growing railway network. He bought a house in Norwich in 1841 and in 1844 he became the owner of Somerleyton Hall, redesigning the village (see p. 55); at the same time he bought Lowestoft harbour for £12,500 – a bargain price even then!

An earlier venture involving the harbour proved unsuccessful; it aimed to create a connection between Reedham on the River Yare and Lowestoft to attract water-borne traffic from Norwich and perhaps compete more favourably with Great Yarmouth

The New Cut reached Haddiscoe, where the artificial waterway joined the river Waveney. Oulton Dyke was widened and deepened to allow ships to reach Oulton Broad more easily; from there they would go through Mutford Lock to Lake Lothing on the seaward side and into Lowestoft harbour.

As so often happened in the nineteenth century, each development was soon outdated; so it was with river traffic. The coming of the railways and the vast increase in east coast fishing especially for herring were good for each other. When Peto opened his Lowestoft to Beccles railway in 1859 he made it possible to send fish quickly and cheaply to the huge London market.

'Peto' land in south Lowestoft, part of the development that attracted railway holiday makers and affluent residents.

Oulton Broad is the only broad in Suffolk, and is equally popular with yacht owners and passengers on the cruise boats.

Power boat racing on Thursday evenings in the summer and at weekends is spectacular and attracts large crowds to the broad.

By then hundreds of drifters were working out of Lowestoft and needed more harbour space, especially in the autumn when the Scottish boats joined them. This was 'time' for herring, and work on the farms being slack, there were plenty of men from nearby villages anxious to find work in the fishing. The harbour was now playing a vital part in making Lowestoft prosperous.

Peto became a public figure of importance; not only becoming MP for Norwich, he contributed financially to the Great Exhibition in 1851 and towards the building of a railway in the Crimea during the war there. For that he was granted a baronetcy. He saw Lowestoft's prosperity relying not only on its fishing industry, but also as a holiday resort. For that he set about creating an amenity south of the river; the beach, Marine Parade, hotels, gardens and the Wellington Esplanade. Although some of his buildings such as St John's Church and the Royal Hotel have now gone and a number of houses were destroyed in both World Wars, it is still very much 'Peto Country'. His success can be measured by the fact that in the post-war days of the 1950s some twenty-five trains each way ran on Saturdays in the summer between Liverpool Street and Lowestoft.

Many of the passengers would have been bound for holiday camps nearby (there were even Holiday Camp Expresses) as well as for the town itself; holiday styles are different today, sad to say.

Peto's work also served to divide Lowestoft into two; the bridge marks clearly North and South Lowestoft, the old and the new. When shipping passes through in and out of the inner harbour it still gives an excuse for being late at work: 'Bridge off.' The only other bridge at Oulton Broad is so far away as to make little contribution to solving the problem.

Peto's railway station, still bearing the name 'Lowestoft Central' was completed in 1854; imposing, it was probably the work of John Thomas, the architect for Somerleyton. One wonders what Peto would have said and done if he had heard of the proposal in 2007 to demolish the building and move the station 400m to the west. That would take it to the footplate men's area; the top of Denmark Road was home for numbers of them who had allotments across the road. They only had to walk through their gardens and across the tracks into the engine shed. How life changes!

The Fishing Industry

In the peak years of the 1950s catches were enormous and so was the fishing fleet. A catch of 200 crans was not unusual: a cran consisted of 28st of fish, and there were probably 1,300 fish per cran.

Lowestoft men had always gone fishing, originally from the beach in quite small boats, but as populations grew they demanded more food and the developing transport system made it possible to move fish to distant towns. Lowestoft Harbour came into use in the nineteenth century for sailing luggers, able to go further and bring back larger catches; soon steam power revolutionised herring fishing as drifters with huge drift nets began to create a new industry.

By 1914 there were 350 Lowestoft drifters joined by 420 from Scotland for the autumn fishing season: no wonder that by the Second World War the North Sea was being over-fished!

Even more damage to fish stocks came with the introduction of trawlers to the fleet powered by diesel engines; they pulled a large wide-mouth net along the sea bed over longer distances. Trawlers were not dependent on the arrival of the shoals of herring in spring and autumn, but fished the year round, bringing in plaice, cod, halibut and sole; on board the crew would gut the fish and pack them in ice ready for sale on arrival at the Trawl Market.

Such was the size of the fishing industry that shipbuilding also became a major source of employment in Lowestoft. Richards and Brooke Marine were the largest companies. Work in their yards meant that the inner harbour became as busy as the trawl basin. A familiar feature of the herring season was the arrival of the Scottish fishergirls who followed their fleet south until the 1950s to gut the herring. Once the herring had disappeared so did they.

But there was other work at Lowestoft: fish had to be cured and smoke houses multiplied to provide the kippers and bloaters that had become popular.

To produce kippers, herrings are opened up, gutted, placed in brine, dried on racks and smoked in the fumes of burning shavings, preferably of oak or ash. Bloaters are smoked as whole herrings; and because they need a steady heat the smoke is produced from oak billets rather than shavings. Few smoke houses are left and the smell of kippering has almost disappeared in Lowestoft Quite apart from the seasonal work that brought the Scottish fishergirls to Lowestoft, herring fishing provided steady employment for women in net making and repair. Net making is known as 'braiding', carried out with a braiding needle: the workers are known as 'braiders', although there are still inshore fisherman who can make their own nets. A block called a 'shale' is held in the left hand to control the size of the mesh, while the braiding is done with the right. Net menders are called 'beatsters'. The work of the braiders and beatsters demands great care and delicacy; contrast that with the feverish and back-breaking work of the 'lumpers', who unloaded the catch from the newly-arrived boats.

Everything depended on marketing the fish and getting it away without delay; the boats were refuelled while the crews saw home again for a few hours. Whatever the job being done, it was hard earned.

Visit *Mincarlo* in Lowestoft Yacht Harbour from Easter to the end of October between 10 a.m. and 3 p.m. Admission is free. She is the last East Anglian Side Trawler, launched by Brooke Marine in 1961; unlike more modern vessels she was known as a side-winder because her nets went over the sides. She is the last of her kind, the one survivor built in Lowestoft with an engine also built in the town. She carried a crew of eleven.

Mincarlo fished until 1975, mainly for cod, plaice, haddock, skate and sole and was among the top half dozen vessels in the fishing fleet. She was later converted as a rig stand-by vessel in the North Sea gas fields; eventually she became redundant when she was bought for preservation by the Lydia Eva Trust.

Lowestoft Porcelain

Now rare and very costly, examples of this lovely product are hard to find. A fine collection can be seen at Lowestoft Museum at Broad House, Oulton Broad: the only larger collections are at the British Museum and Norwich Castle Museum.

More than 100 miles from other and larger producers at Bow, Chelsea, Derby and Worcester, the factory at Lowestoft opened in 1757 following the discovery of deposits of fine white clay by Hewling Luson on his estate at Gunton Hall.

There appears to have been opposition from the established companies and there were rumours of trade secrets being 'acquired', but by 1760 blue and white porcelain was being advertised for sale over the name of Walker & Co.

For some years blue painting was the company's sole decoration and consisted of garden scenes, flowers and birds. Later developments included transfer printing to reduce costs and the use of metallic oxides for the production of 'polychrome' wares. The later colourful products such as teapots continued the floral type decoration and introduced a new oriental 'Mandarin' series of patterns.

A floral decoration on a Chinese theme which included peony illustrations became known as Redgrave patterns from the name of the factory painters who produced them.

A speciality of the Lowestoft factory was the production of birth tablets, small round tablets giving a child's name and birth date on one site and a floral decoration on the other. The factory also became well known for its named and dated pieces, specially ordered. By 1800 the factory had closed: various reasons have been put forward for this, none conclusive. Most likely is a combination of financial trends that offered better returns in other forms of business.

But all has not been lost: with the establishment of Lowestoft Porcelain in 2000, hand painted porcelain has returned to Lowestoft. Traditional colours are being used and of special interest are birth tablets in the style of the original.

The company's workshop and gallery is on Battery Green Road close to the roundabout leading to Whapload Road. The designs, colours and skilled hand painting make the products worthy successors of those from the factory of 1760.

Contact details:

Broad House Museum	Nicholas Everitt Park, Oulton Broad	01502 511457
Lowestoft Porcelain	Battery Green Road, Lowestoft	01502 572940

St Margaret's Church

As part of a continuing campaign to remind everyone that Lowestoft is the most easterly town in Britain, the weathercock on St Margaret's Church lays claim to be the first object to catch the rays of the morning sun. Tower and spire rise to over 120ft, certainly well above any other building. The spire was originally of timber clad with lead, replaced in 1954 with a copper covering.

In spite of its spire and the church's size – it is 184ft long – St Margaret's is not easily seen. It stands over a mile from the lighthouse, well out of town, just off the road to Oulton Broad and Somerleyton, partially hidden by trees. Once seen though, it is clearly a Suffolk church with extensive use of flint and outstanding flushwork on the tower battlements and on the south porch. Within, the local 'hall' style, lacking a chancel arch, gives St Margaret's one more family resemblance with many others in East Anglia.

The church is in the Perpendicular style, dating from about 1480, though the tower is earlier. What makes St Margaret's different and special it is very much a church of the sea; in past days there was always a Harvest of the Sea service to give thanks for the gift of fish, but that no longer takes place. What has remained is the Fisherman's Memorial along the north wall of the nave, giving the names of fishermen from Lowestoft lost at sea between 1860 and 1923. The number is dreadful and when space ran out the memorial was closed and names after 1923 were recorded at the Lowestoft Sailors' and Fishermens' Bethel.

Beyond the screen at the east end of the north aisle is the war memorial chapel with the names of 7,111 men lost in the First World War. Near the screen are more memorials: one commemorates the frigate HMS *Lowestoft*, others remember the lives of those who fell in the Second World War and those who served in the Royal Naval Patrol Service in that war. The people of Lowestoft have paid a heavy price.

At the east end of the church is a fine altar by Sir Ninian Comper of 1905 and a magnificent east window of 1891. A sanctuary bell used during Communion services is, appropriately, a ship's bell. The octagonal font must have been very beautiful before its mutilation during the Commonwealth period; the figures were almost obliterated.

The long length of the church roof, restored in 1899 is impressive and has hammer and tie beams. In the chapel on the south side of the church you may well have a glimpse of crossed keys; the altar was brought from St Peter's in north Lowestoft along with other relics when that church closed.

Opposite St Margaret's are Church Green bungalows for elderly people; it is good to think that although the Fishermen's Almshouses that once stood in Whapload Road, part of the Beach Village were demolished, these have been built to serve a similar purpose. They were opened in 1966.

Directions to St Margaret's Church:

A12 to Lowestoft, then follow A12 north to A12/A1144 roundabout
Keep left on St Peter's Street then turn right (Oulton and Somerleyton) on B1074 into Boston Road and Church Road
St Margaret's Road is on the offset junction with Rotterdam Road
Parking can be found by the lychgate

Felixstowe

Local people are fond of saying that there are two Felixstowes: an Edwardian seaside resort with a spa pavilion and promenade and the Port of Felixstowe that embraces a vast container terminal, cranes and giant ships from world wide ports. This is a huge contrast, but there is also 'Old Felixstowe' and Felixstowe Ferry, yet another world that should not be forgotten.

It is situated only twelve miles from Ipswich, the county town, with a south-facing beach and sheltered by low cliffs and Felixstowe grew quickly from an unimportant fishing village to today's resort when the railway came, attracting day trippers from Ipswich and holidaymakers from far afield. Ipswich grew too, in the nineteenth century, but Felixstowe grew faster than any other town in the region.

The long promenade, extensive gardens, hotels and other large houses on the cliffs gave an atmosphere of elegance; together with the Spa Pavilion they contributed much to Felixstowe's

North of the town, Felixstowe Ferry has fine views of Bawdsey Manor, especially from the river bank, and the Victoria pub.

becoming a flourishing family holiday resort. The mild climate encouraged the growth of a 'convalescent' nursing home business in the town.

River estuaries north and south of Felixstowe made its coastline very vulnerable historically to raiders and settlers from continental Europe; even the powerful Roman occupying army decided it needed to defend what it called the Saxon Shore. Forts were built in Norfolk (Burgh Castle) and near Felixstowe (Walton Castle); sadly, an even more powerful enemy, the sea, destroyed their Walton Castle, which is now under water. It stood at the north end of today's Felixstowe: an engraving of 1786 shows stone fragments on the beach and in the sea, with the Deben and the cliffs of Bawdsey in the background further north.

To have any chance of seeing any of the castle's remains above water, you would need to watch during a very low tide such as in the autumn. Given the right day and time you should be on the sea front at the 'dip' close to the ice-cream kiosk; the Pines, (a road turning) is a good landmark. Focus about 200yds from the sea's edge.

Landguard Fort

It was only when there was a danger of invasion in the sixteenth century that the next serious attention was given to fortifying the coast near Felixstowe. Since then for over 400 years there has been an artillery fort on Landguard Point. Updated and strengthened from time to time, particularly during two world wars, the outline of the main defence consisted of five continuous walls of which three survive, also four heavy bastions designed to fire forward and along the walls to protect an outer ditch. Within the walls is the keep, stone built and heavily protected; an armoured casement held a battery of seven guns. A casement on the south east curtain has a replica gun to show its great size: 12.5in with a weight of 38 tons. The magazines were close to the batteries, designed, protected and laid out carefully to avoid an explosion in the ammunition. Gun emplacements round the curtain walls made Landguard an immensely powerful fort, but like all the other types of static defences, lost its importance with the development of new weapons and the use of air power.

To the rear of the keep are the barrack rooms, officers' quarters on the first floor and soldiers' room below; a parade ground is at the very centre, entered through an arch from the outer passage between the keep and the curtain wall.

Landguard Fort was built to protect the deep-water estuaries of the Orwell and Stour against invasion by sea.

Allow time to visit the keep and to go round the curtain wall to look at the bastions. The views are tremendous; the Harwich bastion looks out on to the Port of Felixstowe with its ships, containers and cranes. Once lonely, situated on an inhospitable, wind-swept shingle bank and flooded from time to time, Landguard Fort now has the port as a modern neighbour.

It would have been interesting to be able to see the painting of the fort by Thomas Gainsborough at the request of the then Governor, Philip Thicknesse, in 1753. Unfortunately it was destroyed by damp. Thicknesse went to see Gainsborough at his Ipswich studio and they became close friends; he always claimed it was his influence that persuaded Gainsborough to move to Bath where he became famous.

One of Gainsborough's first portraits there was of Ann Ford, a beautiful amateur musician who later married Thicknesse; some of the ladies of the day thought that Gainsborough portrayed her too boldly (see Gainsborough p. 154).

Felixstowe Ferry

Facing Bawdsey at the mouth of the River Deben it is truly a different world.

Directions:

At the A14 turn off to the port, and continue on to A154 towards the town
Go forward on the roundabout into Grove Road
Forward again into Colneis Road that skirts Old Felixstowe
Left into winding Ferry Road which passes alongside Felixstowe Golf Course

Among the haphazard collection of holiday bungalows, working huts and waterside clutter at Felixstowe Ferry are places to eat and to buy fresh fish, and also a good parking area close to the road's end.

Sailing is the main attraction, but anywhere near the water is 'heaven' for children, who find crabbing near the ferry slipway a great occupation. There are two good pubs: the Ferry Boat Inn and Victoria, which is close to a Martello Tower (the Ferry Tower). The upstairs dining room there has fine views of the river mouth and Bawdsey Manor across the Deben estuary. The ferry crosses the river to Bawdsey Quay regularly.

Close to Felixstowe Ferry is one of the many Martello Towers, built as protection against a Napoleonic invasion that never came.

The view of heavily laden container ships making their way towards the Port of Felixstowe is unforgettable. Their great stacks of containers reach skywards creating an irregular, aggressive outline, just as if the skyline of Manhattan was sailing by.

Directions:

Felixstowe: Take the A14 and A12 to Ipswich
A14 to Felixstowe Follow docks or town signs at the main roundabout
Felixstowe Ferry direction as above

Adnams' pubs:

Black Tiles	Black Tiles Lane, Martlesham	01473 624038
Half Moon	303 High Street, Walton	01394 216009

Woodbridge

Easy sailing up the River Deben must have been a great relief to early invaders and Woodbridge at the head of navigation would have become an obvious place to settle, set up a market and build a port. Until ships became too large and of deeper draught than the Deben could take, ships at Woodbridge quay were busy with cargoes such as timber, salt and cheese. A flourishing shipbuilding industry grew up, together with the making of sails and ropes.

Boat building today is for leisure craft; yachting is big business after all, there are few stretches of river anywhere to match the beauty of the Deben that includes Waldringfield and Ramsholt. The mouth of the river is worth a visit even if you are not a boat person; you can reach it by road from Bawdsey or Felixstowe Ferry and cross by the pedestrian ferry there.

Always a traffic nightmare because of the narrow thoroughfare which once carried the A12 through the town, Woodbridge had a bypass before the Second World War. However, it remains a busy shopping centre with the railway (sadly) alongside the quay; crossing the line by the footbridge shows the riverside, especially the Tide Mill at its very best.

The Tide Mill is beloved of artists and photographers and is open to the public daily from May to September. Rightly famous, it worked by tidal power until 1957, the last mill in the country to do so. It dates from the 1790s, although a tide mill was recorded here in 1170; a marina took over the mill pond in recent years, but a new, smaller pond has been created. A new 20-ft diameter water wheel has been made and can be seen turning on most open days. Like all good ideas, that of a tide mill is amazingly simple: water is allowed to fill the pond at high tide and when the tide turns the lock gates are closed and water from the pond is passed through the mill to drive the wheel. A second mill at Woodbridge is driven by the wind and is known as Buttrum's Mill from the name of the family who worked it for nearly sixty years until it closed in 1928. Built in 1836, it is one of England's finest tower mills and stands over 60ft high; brick built, it has six floors, four sails and a six-bladed fantail used to turn the main sails into the wind. From the A12 bypass, the Grundisburgh Road gives easy access to the mill and there is a small car park close to it; alternatively walk from Market Hill up Theatre Street past Woodbridge School entrance. The mill is on the other side of the road.

Market Hill is a good starting point to explore the town and St Mary's Church is just a few yards away as Seckford Street leads north towards Great Bealings. The church is one of Suffolk's fine examples of flushwork decoration, both on the tower and the north porch; the base of the porch which dates from 1455 has flushwork panels, battlements and pinnacles. The roof has alternate hammer beams and tie beams; on the north side of the chancel is a monument to Thomas Seckford, who died in 1587. The Seckfords were 'big' in Woodbridge: Thomas established almshouses in Seckford Street and their nineteenth-century successors remain, as does the Seckford Foundation, still serving the town. On the west side of the A12 near Great Bealings is Seckford Hall, the family home built in 1585 and now a country house hotel.

The church has a fine memorial also to Geoffrey Pitman who died in 1627, showing his family all kneeling. The multi-coloured font cover is a beautiful example, but if you want to see the best font cover in the country (some authorities would say in the world), you only have to go a little way out of town on the B1438 through Melton to Ufford.

Keep right on Yarmouth Road through the village: do not join the A12. The church is on the right and you can park close by. The story goes that the font cover was saved because the

The Market Hill has the Shire Hall and
St Mary's Church as close neighbours. The porch
is memorable, with its flushwork decoration.

A short walk west from Market Hill takes visitors to Buttrum's Mill, a fine restored windmill regularly open to the public.

churchwardens refused to let Dowsing's men, charged with destroying any imagery, into the church. It rises 18ft above the font, almost to the roof, each of its tiers receding so that like a graceful spire it soars to an apex, where there is a Pelican in her Piety. At each level are canopies, rich carvings, pinnacles and crocketing; it was once gilded and colourful, but little evidence of that can be seen. For visitors with a practical turn of mind, the lower section can be raised outside the rest so that the font can be used in the normal way. Not to be missed!

Returning to Woodbridge and the work of Thomas Seckford, admire the red-brick Shire Hall on Market Hill which he had built in 1575. The ground floor was originally open and used as a market, the first floor being used as a court house. The hipped roof, Dutch style gables and outside stairs probably date from about 1700. The building is used today by the Woodbridge Town Council and on the first floor is the Suffolk Punch Heavy Horse Museum.

Suffolk Punch Heavy Horse Museum Opening Hours:

From Easter to the end of September on Tuesdays:
Thursdays and Saturdays 2 p.m. to 5 p.m.
Information 01394 380643

Visitors are inevitably drawn to the river; apart from the yachting activity, the railway station, the Riverside Theatre, swimming pool, community hall and Tourist Information Centre are all there. But do not forget one of the best walks: past the Cruising Club, Rowing Club and the Yacht Club and onwards with views down river and across to the open east bank.

In the distance is Martlesham Creek with historic Kingston on its north; it was an ancient royal manor from which Kyson Hill took its name. Kyson Hill is a National Trust area of 4 acres and worth a visit just to see the view from Kyson Point.

Directions to Kyson Hill:

Take Station Road B1438 towards Ipswich
Turn left on Sandy Lane
Turn left again Broomheath over the railway

Directions to Woodbridge:

Take the A12 (Woodbridge bypass)
Access on Ipswich Road B1438 and Grundisburgh Road B1079
Parking at Quayside, Market Hill and elsewhere

Adnams' pubs:

Kings Head	Market Hill, Woodbridge	01394 387750
Cherry Tree	73 Cumberland Street, Woodbridge	01394 382513 (Accomm)

Ipswich

(Variously: *Gipeswic, Gippeswic, Gippeswich, Gippeswyk*)

With comparatively few surviving ancient buildings, Ipswich seems to lack the appearance of an early history. Yet as far back as the seventh century it was an important North Sea trading port and settlement. It is no coincidence that the burial place of the Wuffinga dynasty, Sutton Hoo, is close by; royal trade was doubtless responsible for Ipswich's early waterborne traffic.

From the seventh to the ninth centuries Ipswich pottery could be found all over East Anglia, well before Thetford ware became known; other crafts that served domestic needs included weaving, metalworking and fishing.

Like other east-coast towns Ipswich was vulnerable to attacks from the sea, principally by the Vikings; banks and ditches were the earliest protection. Only in medieval times might walls have been built; Tower Ramparts Shopping Centre and Westgate Street are evidence of this. By the 1790s the North and West Gates had been demolished; both Northgate and Westgate Streets remain.

It was in the Middle Ages that Ipswich grew in some size and importance; as a centre of a large agricultural area, the town also stands at the highest point of navigation at all tides of the River Orwell which joins the Stour estuary at Harwich. Today Parkeston Quay handles North Sea ferries to the Hook of Holland, Denmark and Norway.

During the 'golden years' of the cloth trade, wool, cloth, sheepskins, and leather were major exports, with building stone, salt and wine being imported. After the collapse of the cloth trade Ipswich declined. It took the development of a local industry to manufacture agricultural machinery and an increase in yields from the land to restore prosperity. Milling and malting became important industries, with brewing beginning to need large quantities of barley either locally grown, or brought coastwise from sources such as Norfolk.

Ipswich had a number of monastic houses such as Blackfriars in medieval times, but after the Dissolution and a rebuilding of the town in the sixteenth century its character and appearance began to differ from that of Bury St Edmunds and Norwich.

Many medieval churches survive, but that apart, modernisation took priority over preservation. There are some splendid examples of timber framed buildings in Silent Street and Northgate Street, but little to show otherwise of Ipswich's early history. The Tudor Christchurch Mansion is a splendid and outstanding exception. (see p. 40)

Wolsey's Gateway, College Street

Rare indeed it is for the son of a local butcher to rise to the dizzy heights of the position of Lord Chancellor of England and Cardinal Archbishop of York. In Thomas Wolsey's case he served Henry VIII, a powerful master whose will had to be obeyed – a dangerous combination.

Thomas' birthplace is identified by a plaque in Silent Street, Ipswich, but the only building that marks his rise to fame in his home town is Wolsey's Gateway in College Street, now a commercial route to the docks.

He was clearly a gifted young man whose parents ensured him a successful future by enrolling him at Magdalen College Oxford at the age of eleven. With his intellectual and personal qualities his future in the church was certain; he was noticed by King Henry VIII who was pleased to take into his service someone who would deal with tedious affairs of government on his behalf. By 1514, at the top of the diplomatic ladder and charged with fulfilling the King's wishes, his role as European peacemaker led him to arrange the great meeting known as the Field of the Cloth of Gold in 1520.

His downfall was not far away: in 1527 Henry decided that he wanted his marriage to Catherine of Aragon, his elder brother's widow annulled. This became Wolsey's responsibility; success would allow Henry to marry Anne Boleyn, but the Pope's agreement on divorce was elusive. Wolsey felt the King's anger and lost his post as Lord Chancellor; Parliament agreed to make Henry head of the Church in England. The Reformation had begun.

Wolsey was arrested on his way to York and, intended for execution, died of fever at Leicester Abbey on his way back to London.

During his great days Wolsey obtained Royal approval in 1528 to build a college at Ipswich on the site of the former Priory of St Peter and St Paul. It was intended to be on the model of Cardinal College that had already been established at Oxford.

On College Street stands the sad surviving fragment of Thomas Wolsey's ambitious project that was only partly completed at the time of his disgrace and fall from the King's favour in 1529.

We know that the College's buildings were of stone, although his gateway, now in the town's commercial district is of brick with tall, powerful buttresses. Above the Tudor doorway are two niches, one on each side of Wolsey's weather-worn coat of arms: so little to show his fellow citizens of Ipswich of the glory days when his word was law.

The Old Custom House

A short walk north of the river along the waterfront from Stoke Bridge leads to the Wet Dock and the town's commercial quays with their mills and warehouses. Off to the south is the New Cut, the continuation of the river.

On the common quay (with Key Street behind) is the imposing Old Custom House built by local architect John Medland Clark in 1844/45, whose design unusually incorporated red and yellow brick.

Wolsey's connection with Ipswich would pass unnoticed were it not for the gateway to his college, left unfinished at his downfall.

In classical style with a great portico of four columns supporting a high pediment, this is the most impressive building on the waterfront. Behind and below the external Italianate stairs is a Waterfront Conference Centre manned by members of the Ipswich Maritime trust who have an exhibition of maritime history. It is open on Saturdays and Sundays 11 a.m. to 4 p.m.

The area beyond the Old Custom House has been extensively redeveloped: hotels, apartments and university buildings are making it one of 'the places to be' in Ipswich.

Ipswich: Unitarian Meeting House, Friars Street

Often described as one of Ipswich's architectural gems, its builder in 1699 was Joseph Clarke, listed as a carpenter. Timber-framed and plastered, the house has a red-tiled and hipped roof; its symmetrical front presents itself to perfection. There is a classical style pedimented door at either end; above each is an attractive oval window.

Between the doors are three windows repeated above between the ovals, making five in all on the second storey. Light must have been a vital part in the design of the house as numbers of windows feature on all sides; at the rear they are a tall arched shape with the pulpit in front of them. This must have been intended as a focal point, with fine pulpit carving in the style of Grinling Gibbons and prominent curved stairs.

The candelabra are seventeenth-century Dutch and the box pews are original. Although evidence is lacking, the four great wooden pillars are always said to have been ships' masts.

Opening times:

Saturdays 10 a.m. to 6 p.m.
Sundays 12 noon to 4 p.m.

The Ancient House, Buttermarket

Seen surrounded by nineteenth and twentieth-century buildings of all kinds, particularly by its near-neighbour the Buttermarket Shopping Centre, the Ancient House stands out as a spectacular survivor of a long bygone age, one of which Ipswich is rightly proud.

Old Custom House. (Image supplied by the Port Authority)

The Unitarian Meeting House, close to the bus station, is one of the town's historic and architectural treasures.

The use of light behind the pulpit and its importance make a visit to the interior of the Unitarian Meeting House a vivid experience.

As an example of the craft of pargetting, the external plaster decoration on timbered houses, characteristic of East Anglia, it stands supreme.

When it was built (and extended by successive owners) the house was that of prosperous tradesmen, the locality of the town being that of the fish market. As to the date and the builder's name there is speculation, but a Great Hall with a fifteenth-century hammer-beam roof is the oldest part of the house and we do know that George Copping, a fishmonger bought it in 1567. He was also a draper, became very wealthy and extended the property, probably by adding a Tudor gallery.

On Copping's death his widow sold the house which, in 1591 was sold again, this time to the Sparrowes, who were to own it for over 300 years; even today the Ancient House is recalled as Sparrowe's house by some local observers.

Over those 300 years many changes to the house took place, reflecting the tastes of the time, some revealed when a major restoration took place following the purchase of the house by Ipswich Borough Council in 1979.

The timbered features of the sixteenth-century Ancient House were remarkable in themselves: carved pillars supported the first floor and the long gallery looked down on a courtyard. The open roof had a plaster ceiling inserted; a customary practice that gave extra space above the Great Hall and made the house considerably warmer.

The creation of a first floor room some 40ft long with fine panelling and four oriel windows was part of the last extension to the house along the Buttermarket (formerly the fish market).

It is that extension which is so well recognised today, decorated as it is with extravagant pargetting. In the centre is the coloured coat of arms of Charles II, which gives a date for the pargetting, if not for the extension itself. He visited Ipswich in 1668, although there is no evidence that he hid in the house while 'on the run' after the Battle of Worcester.

The amazing pargetting, the most ambitious in the country, is so heavy that it could almost be called sculpture. Between the ground floor and first floor windows are designs symbolic of the continents known to the craftsmen when the work was done: an Indian with a bow and

Ipswich's Ancient House, now in the care of the borough council, is a spectacular example of East Anglian pargetting; it is still a shop.

Apart from the exterior of the Ancient House, there are excellent examples of pargetting within, especially in the courtyard.

arrow for America, a female figure holding a lamp and staff for Asia, a man sitting and holding an arrow for Africa and for Europe a crowned female figure holding the sceptre of authority. For the fifth window they had no continent and used the figure of Atlas supporting the world.

Look for the elaborate carving on the corner post of the Ancient House and do not miss the side of the building on St Stephens's Lane where the theme of the pargetting is that of shepherds and a shepherdess with a lamb. Above is an agricultural scene which includes a milk churn and other domestic items in the form of a garland.

St Stephen's Lane is also important for a fine view of the church tower north across the Buttermarket. This is St Lawrence on Dial Lane and shows East Anglian flushwork to perfection.

Now see the recommended walk to Christchurch Mansion.

Christchurch Mansion and Park

If you have been visiting the Ancient House in the Buttermarket and have not planned to walk afterwards to Christchurch Mansion, now is the time to do so: it is one of the best history walks in Ipswich:

Leaving the Ancient House, turn right and go for a few steps to Upper Brook Street, turn left to the junction of Tavern Street and Carr Street. There, on the left, is the Great White Horse Hotel, made famous by Charles Dickens, whose remarks in *Pickwick Papers* about it infuriated the landlord. Remember the scandalous episode when Mr Pickwick went into the lady's bedroom by mistake?

Continue across the junction into Northgate Street. The County Library is on the right and almost opposite is the large brick-arched gateway that once led to Archdeacon Pykenham's former mansion; he was archdeacon of Suffolk in 1471 and rector of Hadleigh. (see Hadleigh Deanery Tower p. 99)

Look for a lovely fifteenth-century timber-framed house, once an inn, on a corner on the left; it has ornate carving on the corner post. More noticeable is the Bethesda Baptist

The Great White Horse Hotel
at the corner of Tavern Street
awaited a buyer in 2008. Mr
Pickwick knew it well.

Northgate Street, close to the
Great White Horse Hotel, has
the imposing gateway to the
former residence (1471) of
Archdeacon Pykenham.

Chapel with a four-column portico that stands on St Margaret's Plain and faces down Northgate Street.

Of the many of the town's medieval churches, St Margaret's is the most interesting and attractive. Its flushwork decoration especially on the roof line and the clerestory is a work of art; within, the decoration is of the same quality and there is a fine double hammer-beam roof.

Christchurch Mansion a handsome E-plan red-brick house stands on the site of the former Priory of the Holy Trinity. After the Dissolution it was bought by Paul Withypoll, a London merchant: his son Edmund built the mansion between 1548 and 1550. His daughter inherited the house, which passed to her husband, Leicester Devereux; it was sold in 1735 to Claud Fonnereau, a London merchant descended from a Huguenot family.

When the mansion came up for sale it was bought by Felix Thornley Cobbold and presented to the town on condition that Ipswich Corporation purchased the enormous park for public use. In the heart of the town, it is a blessing for the people of Ipswich. The mansion suffered a fire in the seventeenth century; the roof was raised afterwards and the 'Dutch style' gables were added. Alterations to the entrance porch were made and extensions constructed to the front and rear late in the century.

Visitors enter through the Great Hall which has a black and white chequered floor and, on the west side, an arcaded gallery. Period rooms have been furnished to show how the house would have looked in its early days.

A printed guide and commentary list the rooms open to the public, drawing attention to those which should not be missed; these include the galleries showing the fine art collections.

The art collections include fine pieces of Lowestoft Porcelain (see p. 28) but many visitors go to the mansion because of the Wolsey Art Gallery and John Constable Room, thought to have been used by the Fonnereau family as a dining room. Here you can see Constable's *Mill Stream,* a sketch of Willy Lott's house; his world-famous painting the *The Hay Wain* is a similar scene. Also in the collection are Constable's early *Golding Constable's Flower Garden* and *Golding Constable's Kitchen Garden.*

The Gainsborough collection is of equal importance, as he lived and worked in Ipswich for seven years before finding even greater fame in Bath and London, particularly for his portraiture. However, it was Gainsborough's early landscapes that Constable admired and inspired him to make the countryside, especially the Stour Valley so much loved.

Of Gainsborough's portraits, those of Samuel Kilderbee, town clerk of Ipswich and of his wife Mary, also of William Wollaston are the best known and prized. But do not miss Mrs Bedingfield and her daughter: Gainsborough on her lace is superb.

Other Suffolk painters are well represented, such as Alfred Munnings, George Frost, Thomas Churchyard of Woodbridge and Henry Bright of Saxmundham. A good collection of paintings and water colours by Philip Wilson Steer includes *Knuckle Bones* painted in 1888 at Walberswick. Contemporary painters have good representation too.

Unusual and of special interest are the Hawstead Panels in the Porch chamber, originally at Hawstead Place near Bury St Edmunds. The panels lined a 'painted closet', once an emblematic prayer chamber. It is thought that Lady Drury, who lived at Hawstead Place painted the panels herself prior to 1610, their imagery coming from emblematic books on the subject of spiritual well-being. Each panel has a Latin text at the top and flower paintings at the bottom. Panel 1, for example, is headed (in free translation) 'Unless the Lord build the house, their labour is lost that build it'. At the bottom are paintings of Rosemary and Columbine. An illustrated guide to the panels was published by the Friends of the Ipswich Museums in 2006, available at Christchurch Mansion bookshop.

Christchurch Mansion and Park opening hours:

Tuesday to Saturday 10 a.m. to 5 p.m.
Sunday 2.30 p.m. to 4.30 p.m.
Winter: the Mansion closes at 4.10 p.m.

Christchurch Park Tel: 01473 433989
Tourist Information Tel: 01473 258070

Directions:

From A14 follow Norwich Road and Crown Street past Bus Station
Parking opposite Bus Station and off Fonnereau Road
Park & Ride Service 801 (Bury Road) stops on Northgate Street opposite the Library (12 minute ride)
Also Park & Ride from A12

Adnams' pubs:

County	29 St Helens Street, Ipswich	01473 255153
Duke of York	Woodbridge Road, Ipswich	01473 257115
Greyhound	Henley Road, Ipswich	01473 252862
Lord Nelson	Fore Street, Ipswich	01473 254072
Black Tiles	Black Tiles Lane, Martlesham	01473 624038
Half Moon	303 High Street, Walton	01394 216009

Newmarket

A look at the county map raises the question of why the town is in Suffolk. It was once in Cambridgeshire and the chalk downland surrounding Newmarket certainly has more in common with the higher ground in Cambridgeshire than that in Suffolk.

As a small settlement, part of Exning parish just to the west, Newmarket took on its name as it began to outgrow its 'parent' village in 1220. Earlier its local administration had already been transferred into Suffolk, where it has remained, perhaps surprisingly.

It has been asserted that Newmarket's great advantage was that it was on the main route from London to Norfolk; in the early days that was so, but it was destined to become a handicap. The growth of modern road transport began to turn Newmarket High Street into a huge traffic jam especially at weekends in the summer. The A14, which now bypasses Newmarket has made life more tolerable for residents and motorists alike.

Approaching Newmarket from Cambridge or the M1 a visitor will be greeted at the A11/A1303 roundabout by the spectacular Millennium Statue, a rearing stallion with its handler, sculpted by Marcia Astor and Allan Sly. It is a remarkable piece of work and is a reminder if that were needed that there are over 4,000 horses in Newmarket; the town has long become the home and headquarters of horse racing and breeding in Britain.

The chalk downland, Newmarket Heath in particular, was popular even in medieval times for competitive horse racing, but royal interest that showed itself during the time of the Stuarts set the town on its road to fame. James I used Newmarket as a means of escape from royal duties in London, although his visits were said to be for hawking and hare coursing; his so called 'palace' was something of a mockery. His son Charles I continued the royal patronage of Newmarket and Charles is credited with the building of a stand to watch the horse racing on the Heath.

Following the Restoration in 1660 Charles II became a regular visitor; his enjoyment of horse racing was such that he and his court moved to Newmarket for race meetings each spring and autumn, now an essential part of the racing calendar. He had a palace built, a surviving part now being occupied by the Tourist Information Centre in Palace Street; across the road are the Palace House Stables, said to be the oldest racing stables in the world.

The aristocracy began to seek property in Newmarket because of the town's royal connection; together with the setting up of the Jockey Club in 1770, the establishment of stud farms round

Visitors to Newmarket are greeted by the millennium statue of a stallion at the Stetchworth roundabout.

Palace House at Newmarket was once Charles II's residence. It is now occupied by the Tourist Information Centre.

Close to Palace House is the home of Nell Gwynn, who was a companion to the king at Newmarket.

the town created a substantial industry organised and serviced to produce the highest quality of bloodstock. The arrival of Tatterstall's in 1884 as an auction house for thoroughbreds made Newmarket the premier venue for buying and selling racehorses in the world. The auction ring is open to visitors.

Because of the number of training yards and horsewalks in the town leading to the Heath's 2,800 acres of training grounds, there is a regular movement of horses starting in the early morning to and from the gallops. Breeding, training and racing now employ thousands in and around Newmarket: trainers, stable boys, grooms and a host of others work in and for the industry. For an overall impression of this unique activity – and sport – a visit to the National Horseracing Museum in Newmarket High Street is strongly recommended.

Mention has already been made of the 'rearing stallion' statue on the roundabout at the Cambridge side of the Heath. A short diversion there (signed) to the National Stud is a special way to begin a visit to the town; it is next to the July racecourse (there are two in Newmarket) and to the historic Devil's Dyke.

This ancient and massive earthwork is thought to have been a defence against attacks from Mercians in the west; it stretches 7½ miles from Reach to Woodditton and there are public rights of way along it. Choose the right spot on a clear day, look north and you can see Ely Cathedral from the top of the bank some 40ft up.

The National Stud is set in 500 beautiful tree-lined paddocks and specially designed buildings; it is the showcase for British thoroughbred breeding.

Incorporating the Wavertree Trust, activities include stallions at stud, equine services, owner breeders' clubs, education and training, public tours and corporate hospitality.

From March to September seventy-five-minute tours by coach and on foot take visitors behind the scenes. Prominent are the stallions at stud: winners themselves, they command fees of many thousands of pounds in the hope that their progeny become champions too. There is also a fascinating opportunity to make close contact with the foals: as yearlings bred at the National Stud they command high prices in the sales ring.

Devil's Dyke at Newmarket, close to the National Stud, offers magnificent views.

Moulton's Pack Horse Bridge just outside Newmarket is a fine, well-preserved example.

Tour bookings for the National Stud:
Tel: 01638 666789

Adnams' pub:

The Castle Inn   Castle Street, Cambridge   01223 353194

Great Houses

Bawdsey Manor

(With acknowledgement to Jane Hart & Alexander's International School)

The arrival at Bawdsey Manor in 1994 of Ann and Niels Toettcher and their successful International School marked a new phase in the life of this unusual house. The School provides high quality English language tuition combined with academic study or sports for young people aged from eleven to eighteen.

From 1936 the house had been highly secret. Bawdsey Manor Research Establishment, was where Sir Robert Watson-Watt experimented on and developed a radar system that was to make victory possible in the Battle of Britain. He showed it was possible to detect aircraft in flight; and a chain of radar stations was set up round the south east coast to give a warning of impending air raids. No wonder it was secret! Bawdsey played a later role as a defence base for a Bloodhound surface to air missile unit but was finally decommissioned in 1991.

Bawdsey Manor began life as the home of William Cuthbert Quilter, who set up the National Telephone Co., later taken over by the GPO in 1912. He acquired 8,000 acres at the mouth of the River Deben, bought the title 'Lord of the Manor' at Bawdsey in 1833 and began to build a holiday home, enlarging it in a mixture of styles as his family grew.

Studying the house from different angles you are reminded of Hampton Court, then of a French style by the white stone West Front – even a hint of the East in the White Tower. Inside, all the principal rooms have richly decorated oak panelling and linen fold abounds. Ceilings are ornate and loosely Louis XVI style. The Great Hall boasts heavy moulded beams, one a pseudo-hammer beam, and a Minstrels' Gallery.

The gardens were created by Lady Quilter in a medley of styles; she had a difficult task on this windswept site, but successfully designed red-brick Italianate terraces. A sunken garden links with other parts of the grounds by grotto-like underground tunnels. There was a boat house (of course) and a tea house on the top terrace. An artificial cliff 50m high provided shelter from those winds.

Today the manor offers guest accommodation with wonderful views over the River Deben, also more modest accommodation in several houses on the site including Beach House. You can be married at Bawdsey Manor, run courses in the house, or join one already set up.

It is a wonderful area for walking, exploration and history: Sutton Hoo is very close, there are castles at Orford and Framlingham and there is access to Havergate Island, the RSPB Nature Reserve they call 'Island of the avocet' on the River Alde.

Viewing:

If you just want to see Bawdsey Manor, the house is open through the Invitation to View Scheme.
Address: Bawdsey Manor, Bawdsey, Suffolk IP12 3AZ
Tel: 01394 411633

The west front of Bawdsey Manor. (Courtesy of the Bawdsey Manor Estate)

The Dragon Tower from the Red Tower. (Courtesy of the Bawdsey Manor Estate)

Directions:

A12 to Woodbridge then A1152 Woods Lane and Wilford Bridge Road
Cross railway and fork right at roundabout to follow B1083
Continue Sutton, Shottisham and Alderton
At Bawdsey keep left to the Manor

Adnams' pubs:

Oyster Inn	Woodbridge Road, Butley	01394 450790
Jolly Sailor	Quay Street, Orford	01394 450243
Kings Head	Front Street, Orford	01394 450271 (Accomm)

Helmingham Hall Gardens

Someone knowledgeable, probably Patrick Taylor, once said 'Few great houses have gardens as exquisite as those at Helmingham'. Like looking at a photograph you wish you had taken yourself, that quote speaks for me, too. But it must be added that it is the complete harmony and unity of the house, the park and the gardens that so affect visitors. Although the house is not open to the public, it is there – an essential feature of the whole.

Look across the Parterre to the west front of the hall, or along the herbaceous border with the house in the distance and the effect is stunning.

The red-brick façade of the moated house conceals a half-timbered building beneath, completed in 1510 by John Tollemache. An earlier house on this site was Creke Hall, the family home of his bride Elizabeth Joyce; the Tollemaches have been here ever since John's days.

The approach to Helmingham Hall gardens takes the visitor immediately into the 400 acre deer park. Car parking is arranged on the right of the drive, beyond the pond and the pedestrian route to the gardens curves behind the Stable Shop and the Coach House tea rooms. By the garden entrance is a fine view of the hall with its moat and bridge.

A second – the garden moat – encloses the Walled Garden, my favourite spot at Helmingham. Cross the Parterre, stop at the hybrid musk roses and pass through the wrought iron gate to see herbaceous borders and flowers like no others.

Roses again: climbers of all varieties and colours and, depending on the season, clematis too. One of the events of the year is the season for sweet peas: they form tunnels of delicate colours and perfume. Borders cross left and right to areas of shrubs, fruit and vegetables; against the walls are seasonal flower borders. The later summer border has nicotiana and shrubs such as viburnum and hydrangea; beyond the walls are the wild flower and orchard gardens.

You need to take your time at Helmingham. Thank goodness for the seats in the gardens, where you can rest and absorb it all before going back towards the house, tea rooms and shop. Even then there is more: turn towards the house and its bridge as you come out of the tea room to see the knot garden and yet more roses.

If you look carefully at the knot garden you will see the 'fret' of the Tollemache coat of arms in two of the beds and their initials in the others. The view across the knot garden towards the roses is extraordinary.

Helmingham Hall Gardens. The house is not open to the public, but the gardens are open at weekends and are a delight, setting a standard for other houses to follow.

Opening times:

Wednesdays and Sundays 2 p.m. to 6 p.m. from early May to mid-September.
Details, including special events from: 01473 890799

Directions:

From Ipswich nine miles
Take the B1077 Debenham Road
From the A14, Stowmarket A1120 tourist route
Beyond Pettaugh turn right on B1077

Adnams' pubs:
Queen's Head	The Street, Brandeston	01728 685307
Gladstone Arms	Combs Ford, Stowmarket	01449 612339

Ickworth (National Trust)

Many people going to Ickworth do so imagining that the house will be another of the great family houses that attract thousands of visitors every year, Their reaction may well be 'incredible', perhaps 'unbelievable'; the builder Frederick Hervey, 4th Earl of Bristol even had to suffer criticism from his wife who called the house 'a stupendous monument of folly'.

He would say (of course) that he was misunderstood: he didn't intend it as a home, but as a showcase for his enormous collection of works of art obtained during his extensive European tours in the eighteenth century. His intention was that the Rotunda should house the family, the curved wings his display galleries; but it all turned out differently.

Just a younger son, Frederick Hervey had only modest prospects until his elder brother was appointed Lord Lieutenant of Ireland and secured Frederick rich archbishoprics there. He was then able to travel and indulge his obsession with collecting which he did with some success;

Ickworth. (NTPL/Andreas von Eisiedel)

when his brother, the 3rd Earl died in 1779, Frederick succeeded to the title, was richer than ever and became known as the Earl Bishop.

With the family estate at his disposal, the Earl Bishop planned his great house, employing Francis Sandys as his architect; by 1795 work on the foundations was in hand, but soon afterwards his art collection was confiscated by a Napoleonic army. He never recovered it, but continued to collect and to work on the house at Ickworth.

If the Earl Bishop's wife was offended by the Rotunda and the sheer size of the new house, she would surely have thrown up her hands in horror at its huge portico, as big as an average house, the entrance hall and the staircase hall. In any event, the Earl Bishop died in 1803 when the Rotunda was unfinished, its completion and building of the wings was undertaken by successive Marquesses of Bristol.

Enormous scagliola columns support the entry to the Staircase Hall (Scagliola is a plaster composition of sand, lime, gypsum and crushed stone to give colour; it was used to face stone columns and highly polished to resemble marble). Beyond the pillars is John Flaxman's marble sculpture *The Fury of Athamas*; above the balcony are *The Last Communion of St Jerome* by J.A. Ribera, *Elizabeth Fulton, Countess of Bristol* and *John 1st Earl of Bristol*, both by Enoch Seeman.

The Dining Room is full of Hervey family portraits and has a magnificent mahogany dining table with twelve chairs; above it is a 30-light chandelier of 1820 that came from the Bristol's house in London.

The Library, largest of the state rooms, has four scagliola columns and handsome rosewood bookcases; the silk curtains were woven by the Gainsborough Silk Weaving Co. of Sudbury. Of the pictures, two of the outstanding examples are *Infanta Balthasar Carlos* by Velasquez, 1635 and *Death of Wolfe* by Benjamin West 1779.

The Drawing Room mirrors the shape of the Dining Room; the Wilton carpet was made for the room and the curtains and upholstery created by the Gainsborough Silk Weaving Co. A set of six gilt armchairs is of the highest quality, also two tables and a writing desk. Do not miss three fine portraits here: *Lady Elizabeth Foster*, daughter of the Earl Bishop, by Angelica Kauffman, *Commodore the Hon. Augustus Hervey* by Thomas Gainsborough and *Augustus Hervey*, also by Gainsborough.

The East Corridor leads to the Smoking Room, where a Hervey Conversation Piece by Hogarth is to be seen, while the West Corridor leads to the Pompeian Room, completed in 1879. The spectacular Italian Renaissance style of painted decoration was the speciality of J.D. Grace, whose work is also on the staircase of the National Gallery in London. It is based on Roman painting discovered at the Villa Negroni near Rome.

From the balcony of the Museum Landing on the first floor are fine views of the Staircase Hall. A collection of fans is on display and in the Museum Room is the Hervey's silver collection that includes complete sets of eighteenth-century dining and dessert plate. A beautifully worked tureen of 1752 and a Baroque wine cistern of 1680 are but two of the wonderful pieces on display.

The West Wing has recently been converted to form a reception area (and ticket office), shop and restaurant. Here, too, is the Orangery; there are facilities there for wedding and banqueting events.

Away to the south of the house a visitors' route leads to the church, walled garden and summer house; to the south-east corner of the park is the Fairy Lake. Close to the house is a raised terrace walk; over a low wall are fine distant views of the Park, while towards the house the Rotunda can be seen through the trees. A long central path bordered by identical clipped bushes leads back to the Rotunda; on the way look for the Silver Garden and Stumpery on the right.

Directions:

Ickworth: A14 to Bury St Edmunds J44 then A134 Rougham Road
Keep right on A1302 Cullum Road to roundabout
Turn left on Out Westgate into Horringer Road
Ickworth 3 miles on right.

Adnams' pubs:

Gladstone Arms	Combs Ford, Stowmarket	01449 612339
Red Lion	School Road, Great Wratting	01440 783237

Kentwell Hall

What is it they say about inspiration and perspiration as essential ingredients when undertaking a new task? When Patrick Phillips acquired Kentwell Hall in 1991 with an ambition to restore it and to recreate its garden he needed plenty of both – passion, too. Fortunately all these years later his vision has not dimmed; his work and that of his wife Judith continue, new ideas are born and more people visit Kentwell.

Kentwell was in a dire condition in 1991 through years of neglect and having been the home successively of ten unrelated families. A serious fire in 1826 had meant both considerable interior restoration and remodelling were needed. Built as an Elizabethan Manor House by William Clopton in about 1540, the central block was followed by two wings some fifty years later, creating the E-plan popular at that time. With a long pedigree like this, repairs to roofing were expected to be necessary and, as always, there were many hidden defects such as dry rot and beetle infestation.

During the summer months outdoor work has been regularly undertaken; evidence of this are the gates themselves, moved and re-erected as a gate screen giving a good view of the house instead of at the far end of the long approach avenue of lime trees. On either side of the gate screen the Phillips built two octagonal pavilions, one serving as a Reception area and ticket office, the other as visitors' toilets.

Seen from the gate screen the beautiful proportions of the house can be appreciated as well as its details, its towers, gables and pinnacles. More than beautiful, Kentwell seen across the moat speaks of peace, quiet and permanence. It has neighbours too – a huge dovecote to the west; with 574 nesting boxes it is thought to be the largest in Suffolk. Also to the west is the Moat House, the oldest building on the site and now identified as a brewhouse; it was probably used for other domestic services too.

Not the least of the surprises at Kentwell is the vast stock of fish in the moat; visitors crossing the bridge stand wide-eyed at the numbers and activity of the fish. In Tudor times they would have provided an essential part of the food supply, particularly in bad harvest years.

Entry to the house is across the courtyard into the west wing which has been least altered by the families who occupied Kentwell during its 500-year life. In the course of restoration of the domestic rooms here in the west wing, Tudor fireplaces and brickwork have been uncovered; panelling has been cleaned and polished and the Housekeeper's Room returned to a suitable use. No doubt as was traditional, the rooms on the ground floor opened into each other; a corridor giving separate access now, leads to the Little Dining Room with Tudor brickwork.

A passage leads into Thomas Hopper's nineteenth-century Dining Room heavily decorated with plaster panelling; spacious and colourful, it is an introduction to the Great Hall which is entered traditionally through the Screens Passage below the Minstrels' Gallery. The high ceiling here accommodates the gallery and there is an abundance of plaster decoration; the great bay windows has some fifteenth-century painted glass and there is a massive eighteenth-century stone fireplace.

Hopper's work continues on the ground floor in the Drawing Room, Billiard Room and the Library where Georgian influence can be seen. In the case of the Library, Hopper made use of Scagliola (an imitation marble surface) for his screen. This was used with great success at Ickworth. (see p. 50) The main staircase close to the exit from the Great Hall is passed to reach these rooms; it dates from about 1675 and leads to a series of rooms of which the State Bedroom, the State Dressing Room and the Victorian Room are of major interest. At the end of the former Long Gallery was the Servants' Dormitory. At this end the back stairs lead down to the passage and Courtyard.

Extensive and successful as the restoration of the house has been the gardens are equally remarkable and a sheer delight. A walk round the east end of the house through the Cedar Lawn follows the line of the moat then turns north to the fabulous walled garden. Now with a Potager and Herb Garden and lined with espalier fruit trees, everything grows to perfection in the warm air that circulates within the walls. It was particularly fortunate to have a visit on Apple Day (30 September), when there was a display of the many varieties of apples in the walled garden and a ready supply of sample pieces of apple. Incredible!

West of the Walled Garden are the Fish Pond and Dovecote and an interesting view of the Moat House. Explore the Wild Garden and Back Moat and look for the Ice House, but allow time to see the farm and animals: cows, pigs and poultry are all there. In the 'Overcroft' upstairs in the Stable Yard is the counter service restaurant. Lasagne and fruit juice never tasted better.

One of the Phillip's imaginative ideas is that of Kentwell's Tudor recreations where visitors meet real people in real clothes engaged in real sixteenth-century activities.

For programme details of events:

Tel: 01787 310207

Directions:
A14 to Bury St Edmunds J44 then A134 south to Long Melford
or
A12 to Colchester then A134 north to Long Melford
or
A1307 from Cambridge then A1092 to Long Melford

Adnams' pubs:

The Bull	The Street, Cavendish	01787 280245
Cock Inn	3 Callis Street, Clare	01787 277391

Euston Hall

In spite of its official address Euston Hall is in Suffolk – just! A few yards north of Euston village along the Thetford road is the bridge over the Little Ouse River and the county boundary. The hall houses an extraordinary collection of royal and family paintings dating back to the time of Charles II and the Restoration that make a visit there a unique experience.

Although there was a manor house at Euston for hundreds of years, it had fallen into serious disrepair when Henry Bennet, Earl of Arlington bought the estate in 1666. He had been appointed Secretary of State to Charles II who had been restored to the throne in 1660; no doubt Arlington wanted to build a house that befitted his position. It was in the grand French style with domes at the four corners.

The Arlingtons had a daughter Isabella who would inherit her father's wealth; this did not escape the notice of the King's principal mistress (he had a number of them!), Barbara Villiers, created Lady Castlemaine and Duchess of Cleveland. Her second son, Henry Fitzroy duly married Isabella; one of his several titles was Duke of Grafton and the family has occupied Euston Hall ever since. Henry died aged only twenty-seven fighting in Ireland and was succeeded by his son Charles who, in 1750 remodelled the house in the later classical style. His architect was Matthew Brettingham, a pupil of William Kent who designed Holkham Hall in Norfolk. The domes were replaced by low pyramid roofs, but many of Brettingham's changes were destroyed by fire in 1902 and some of the rebuilt house was demolished fifty years later.

Not a church tower as it appears to be. It was a mill that provided a water supply for Euston Hall.

The domed temple was intended as a banqueting house.

The main entrance to the hall is now across Brettingham's courtyard and through the stable block. There are many fine pieces of furniture in the house and family belongings of great value and interest, but it is the collection of paintings that makes a visit so exciting.

In the Outer Hall is Van Dyck's painting of Charles I's five elder children, identical to that in Windsor Castle and among those in the Inner Hall is the famous portrait by Sir Peter Lely of King Charles II in his Garter robes, also that by Lely of Barbara Villiers, mother of the First Duke of Grafton seen as the penitent Magdalen.

Of the paintings in the Small Dining Room the famous and contrasting *Mares and Foals* by George Stubbs is accompanied by other Euston landscapes. Over the fireplace is Charles II while still in exile by Philippe de Champaigne; to his left is his mother, Henrietta Maria by Van

St Genevieve's Church of 1676 is set among sheep meadows on the estate.

Euston Hall.

Dyck and to his right is Henrietta (Minette), Charles' favourite sister by Mignard, dressed for a masque.

Further examples of this outstanding collection are along the staircase, part of the original 1670 house; in the Square are Charles Second Duke of Grafton by Van Loo, Barbara Villiers with her son in a Madonna and Child pose by Lely and Van Dyck's famous group of the three eldest children of Charles I (Charles, James and Mary). Be sure to have a house guidebook because of the many paintings in the collection you will want to identify and to recall.

Visitors have much to see in the grounds, laid out by William Kent, John Evelyn and Capability Brown. King Charles'; gates, built to commemorate a visit by the King connect the formal garden with the Pleasure Grounds, where a tributary of the Little Ouse River still has its watermill of 1670 that looks remarkably like a church. An external restoration was carried out in 2000/2001 and a new waterwheel fitted.

Every great house of the day needed an architectural folly; at Euston it is the octagonal temple of 1746, Kent's last design. It is domed and has a handsome pedimented window set within an arch of rusticated quoins using flint for their effect. The Temple is not open to the public, but the church of St Genevieve is; it replaced the original medieval parish church in 1676.

Prominent over the door is the coat of arms of the First Duke of Grafton and his wife; the woodwork in the church is of the highest quality and is believed to have been designed by Grinling Gibbons. The light from circular clerestory windows and the white interior surfaces focus attention on the arches and vaults: these are superbly decorated with coloured plaster bands.

Directions:

A14/A11 north; pass Barton Mills
At Elveden turn right to Barnham, crossing A134
At A1088 (Euston) turn right

Adnams' pub:

Queen's Head   The Street, Long Stratton   01508 530164

Somerleyton Hall

Although Somerleyton is very close to Lowestoft, that is by no means the only connection with the town. It was Sir Morton Peto, entrepreneur, railway builder and 'developer' of Lowestoft, who bought the 4,500 acre estate and remodelled the former Jacobean manor, transforming it into a Victorian country house of some style. Wealthy enough to buy Lowestoft Harbour, he could afford to employ John Thomas as his architect who worked for many years on the Houses of Parliament: clearly only the best would do! It took from 1844 to 1851 for the work to be completed, only for Peto to fall so seriously into debt that he had to put the estate up for sale in 1861.

Another rich entrepreneur, Sir Francis Crossley, who had made his money manufacturing carpets in Halifax, bought the estate in 1864: his great great grandson Hugh Crossley lives there today, Lord and Lady Somerleyton having retired some years ago. The Crossleys have made alterations, mostly inside the house and to the gardens. Externally, Somerleyton Hall appears much as it was in 1864; a red-brick house with projecting wings; on one side is a campanile tower from which the Crossley flag flies and on the other is a clock tower overlooking the stable block. Decorative use of Caen stone in dressings on the porch and elsewhere and the Dutch style gable ends add to the character of the house.

One of the interior changes took place in 1920 when Peto's Banqueting Hall with its high roof was converted into a Library on the ground floor with bedrooms above. Woodwork housing the 3,500 books was done with a lighter touch than in the Oak Room, for example, where the Jacobean work, though exquisite, seems dark and heavy today. Some of it is attributed to Grinling Gibbons.

Another change was the re-decoration of the Dining Room which adjoins the Library. The delicate coloured plasterwork is in Robert Adam's style with pastel wall colours; the white fireplace and door case with 'broken' pediment are in the restrained classical tradition too. The carpet was specially designed and woven by John Crossley & Sons of Halifax incorporating features of the Somerleyton arms.

Somerleyton Hall.The estate includes Fritton Lake, now developed as a tourist venue. (The Crossley family)

Two paintings of the highest quality are here: 'Ferdinand and Isabella' by Bol, a pupil of Rembrandt and *The Siege of San Sebastian* by Stanfield.

The lighting and richness of the Ballroom make that the gayest of all the rooms at Somerleyton – and so it should, with white and gold its predominant colours and its deep crimson curtains.The ceiling and frieze are in the same luxurious style, the light in the room being magnified by the facing mirrors that have the unusual effect of showing a visitor several images at the same time.

The Staircase Hall has substantial oak banisters, posts and landing gallery; as such an important feature of the house there are Crossley family portraits lining the walls. More overpowering in the Entrance Hall are the two great polar bears, a reminder of a nineteenth-century journey to the Arctic by the first Lord Somerleyton.They stand in the corners against extravagant oak carved walls and doorway. In total contrast is the floor of Minton tiles and a simple 1865 marble figure of a little boy, later to be the 1st Lord Somerleyton with a spade in his hand and shells in his lap.

Although the astonishing Victorian Winter Garden was demolished in 1914, replaced by the Sunken Garden close to the Tea Room, the Paxton glasshouses remain. There are over 12 acres of gardens open, with wonderful trees and shrubs, but most visitors spend some time in the formal garden; from there are fine views of Somerleyton Hall. Along the variety of walks towards the Walled Garden are examples of the statuary once in the Winter Garden.

To the right of the Walled Garden is a 76yd pergola; beyond it is a yew hedge maze, planted in 1846.

Directions:

Somerleyton Hall: A12 to Lowestoft (north)
At roundabout turn left to A1144, then
Fork right B1074 signed Somerleyton
or
From Norwich A146/A143 to St Olaves
Then right on B1074 to Somerleyton

Adnams' pubs:

Butchers Arms	London Road, Beccles	01502 712243
Wherry Inn	The Street, Geldeston, Beccles	01508 518371
Prince Consort	11 Nelson Road, Great Yarmouth	01493 843268

Otley Hall

Be it a car or a sofa, supermarket or skyscraper, size today is everything. Look at the crowded car parks in the summer at Blenheim Palace or Chatsworth for the evidence of that.

Yet there are some houses, smaller and unpretentious that represent tradition in their building styles and have played a part in historic events far beyond their walls. Otley Hall is one of these gems: a Grade I listed Suffolk manor house with moat whose owner was John Gosnold in about 1450. In those early days moats were a protection against intruders; in the course of time they became less necessary for defence, but still continued to have social importance as at Otley, after the western section of the moat had been abandoned or filled in.

The overwhelming impression visitors at Otley have is of the massive, high twin brick chimneys and the timber studding of the Gosnolds' hall; the studs are vertical and close set in the Suffolk style so familiar in the Stour Valley, especially at Lavenham.

Entrance is by the south door through a vestibule; there were once stairs here, leading to a solar and bedrooms, but when this entrance was formed in 1910 the stairs were removed. Before 1910 the house entrance was on the north of the building by the traditional means of the Screens Passage.

John Gosnold's son Robert began building a splendid new wing in about 1480, a Great Hall being its central feature, always a focal point of life in a medieval house. At the western end was a timber screen with two archways that led to the kitchen and buttery in the service area; when fully panelled the screen would have reduced draughts from the outside door which was the main entrance prior to 1910.

When the service wing was demolished and a window was inserted in the new west wall the entrance door was moved 10ft to the east. The Screens Passage lost its original purpose, but remains, a fine piece of history, as do the initials R.G. (Robert Gosnold) in the spandrels of the old north doorway.

The Great Hall seen from the north west is typical Elizabethan in style, jettied out at first-floor level with windows above and below; here the brick nogging between the timber studs is in an attractive herring-bone pattern. Beyond is a band of lovely vine-motif pargetting; on the first floor is the Banqueting Room with handsome wall paintings. The ground floor was open until about 1900; bowls were played and cock fighting took place there; closed in today, there are offices and cellars in this area.

The high quality of the carving of the beams and joists in the Great Hall and its great eight light window added later show how much time and money was spent on it. The timbered chimneypiece is huge and heavily moulded too. Beyond the 'high table' end of the Great Hall is the Linenfold Parlour which has become deservedly famous because of the extent and quality of its linenfold panelling; another huge window here has fourteen lights above the transom and seven below. On the floor above are the solar and the principal bedrooms.

The South Wing has rendered walls and inside a Minstrel's Gallery overlooks the two- storeyed Dining Hall. Surrounding the house are award-winning gardens, a joy in themselves.

Sad to relate, the Gosnolds supported the losing Royalist cause in the Civil War, suffering themselves and ultimately losing the house too. But by then they had already ensured the Gosnolds' place in history through the person of Bartholomew Gosnold, John's cousin and a friend of Walter Raleigh and recently acknowledged as the 'founding grandfather' of America.

It was in the Great Hall at Otley where Bartholomew met Sir Thomas Smythe to seek financial support for an expedition to found a permanent settlement in the New World. In 1606 three small ships under the command of Admiral Christopher Newport: *Discovery*, *Godspeed* and *Susan Constant* made the four month voyage safely and the party settled at Jamestown.

Gosnold had already made an expedition in 1602, charting and naming Cape Cod and Martha's Vineyard, after his daughter who had died in infancy. Bartholomew only survived a few weeks after the arrival in 1607, so Captain John Smith had to assume authority and became Governor of the colony, but it is Gosnold who is remembered as the driving force to found the settlement. The drama of the voyage even impressed Shakespeare, whose description of Prospero's island in the *Tempest* was based on Gosnold's account of New England.

Any visitor to Otley Hall should remember that it was in the Great Hall that plans were laid and decisions taken that would found a settlement in America even before the Pilgrim Fathers made their journey to the New World.

Opening hours:

Otley Hall is open under the Invitation to View programme; in addition pre-booked groups are welcome all-year round and the hall hosts a number of Open Days and Quiet Days.
For further information contact the secretary on 01474 890264 or visit www.otleyhall.co.uk

Directions:

Otley Hall: From Ipswich B1077 via Westerfield
At Ashbocking Green turn right on B1078
At B1079 turn left on Church Road
Fork right in Otley and pass Primary School
Keep left for Otley Hall

Adnams' pubs:

Queens Head	The Street, Brandeston	01728 685307
Kings Head	17 Market Hill, Woodbridge	01394 387750
Cherry Tree	73 Cumberland Street, Woodbridge	01394 382513

Museums and Castles

Stowmarket: Museum of East Anglian Life (MEAL)

If you visit here and expect a building with collections of historic items in glass cases supervised by stern-looking attendants in peaked caps, MEAL will be a wonderful surprise. It consists of 70 acres of farmland displaying a wide variety of activities illustrating aspects of East Anglian life in the countryside.

Just as surprising is the fact that the museum site lies in the centre of Stowmarket, having been placed in trust by the Misses V.M. and E.T. Longe for the development of the museum. It was formerly part of the home farm of Abbot's Hall, still a private residence of the Longes.

There was a danger that life and work in the past would only be seen today through pictures if machinery, tools and buildings were allowed to decay, become ruined and be lost forever. Instead of this, much material, even landmark buildings from all over the region have been brought to the museum, restored and re-erected there. In the care of the museum's conservators they will survive for all time.

Of the original farm, the remaining building is Abbot's Hall Barn, built in the thirteenth century which visitors see first on their tour. It is huge, having been used as a tithe barn to house the tithe (one tenth of peoples' production from the land) paid to the Church in medieval times. The timbering of the interior is exceptional – had it not been it could hardly have survived; time and bad weather always affected such ancient buildings. Horses used to be the mainstay of farm work and some of the Museum's horse-drawn wagons are in the barn.

The first ancient building brought to the site and re-erected was Edgar's Farmhouse from Combs, near Stowmarket. It was part of a larger nineteenth-century farmhouse, but records show that the original was built as far back as the 1350s.

Soon after reaching Edgar's Farmhouse, the site opens up to the eight acre meadow, where there is a Blacksmith's Forge of about 1750 from Grundisburgh and a hurdlemaker's workshop.

The meadow is home to grazing animals: Red Poll cattle and Suffolk sheep and leads down to the small animals' enclosures including goats and pigs beloved of children. On my last visit staff were shearing lambs that were being taken one by one from the family enclosure for it to be done. It was fascinating to see the anxiety of the small flock for the safe return of the last shorn lamb; equally, how readily it returned. Not led by a lead, but by a bottle of milk, impossible to resist. 'They never forget the bottle, however old they are,' said one of the staff.

The Suffolk sheep, Red Poll cattle and the Suffolk Punch work horse are known as 'The Trinity'.

Buildings along the fringe of the meadow include the Mortlock Engineering Workshop of 1920 from Lavenham; the company were blacksmiths and repaired farming equipment, but were contractors too, hiring engines and machinery for farms for seasonal work such as harvesting.

The modern William Bone building houses the Ransomes' exhibition. Opened in 2001, it displays a range of the largest and smallest of Ransomes' products that made the company a household name. An 1803 patented cast-iron ploughshare and equipment for railway construction established the importance of the company in the rural countryside, followed by a steam plough. Look for their steam engine and threshing machine. As Ransomes, Sims and Jeffries they became known to gardeners world-wide in 1832 with the first lawnmower.

The Boby building from Bury St Edmunds came from the biggest factory in the town in the nineteenth century, manufacturing agricultural equipment of all kinds. This included the 'power plants' of yesterday: steam engines that replaced water or wind power for mills and the exciting steam traction engines. The star of the collection is *The Empress of Britain*, built by Charles Burrell of Thetford in 1912. Another famous manufacturer was Garrett of Leiston (see p. 90).

Great machines like *The Empress of Britain* travelled the country roads as if they were steam railways, going from farm to farm on hire for seasonal work, especially at harvest time. Labour was also important: gangs of workers went with them and locals joined the crews. If any older schoolboy was asked in those days when he was leaving school the reply was always 'At harvest'. He would be in the fields too.

In spite of the introduction of steam, much of the heavy work on farms was done by the Suffolk Punch, a gentle giant of a horse. Sadly, few working horses remain on farms now, but there is one at MEAL, a fine example of a great breed. They have enormous drawing power – look at the loads they can pull, even on heavy land! Work on clay is second nature to the Suffolk Punch, its short hairs (feathers) on its legs, rather than the long feathers of other breeds are a great advantage in working conditions in East Anglia. At the southern end of the museum site beyond the small animals' enclosure is the Rattlesden River where there are two treasures not to be missed.

The first of these at the end of Crow Lane and on the riverbank is the Eastbridge wind pump that was brought damaged after a storm from its site near Leiston where it was used to drain the Minsmere levels. It is of the 'smock' design, so-called because it resembled a miller's smock; used to scoop up water from the marshes, allowing it to drain away along a ditch, it reduced the flooding of grazing land.

Built about 1850 and timber framed, it has fully shuttered sails which can be seen turning on a windy day. The mill is smaller than the Herringfleet wind pump on the River Waveney near St Olaves which has cloth spread sails and is preserved by Suffolk County Council (see p. 126). These smock mills were believed to have been invented by the Dutch; they were much fewer in number than the post mills such as that at Saxtead near Framlingham, used for flour milling.

Alton Water Mill, Mill House and Cart Lodge are only a few yards away along the riverbank. They were brought from Stutton near Holbrook just south of Ipswich as a condition of obtaining planning consent for the construction of a reservoir there. A mill pool was created at MEAL and provides water to drive the water wheel and to grind flour (the museum programme gives operating days and times). The mill dates from the mid-eighteenth century and worked until the 1960s.

Close by is Great Moulton Chapel, a rural 'tin tabernacle', non-denominational and evangelical and one of many built at low cost for village congregations.

For visitors who like to see things happening, there are regular demonstrations at MEAL by craftsmen; rooms close to the restaurant illustrate home, school and work at the turn of the century. Friends of the Museum run a shop to raise funds and at the exit is the museum shop and gift centre.

For events leaflet call: 01449 612229

Directions:

To reach MEAL leave the A14 at A1308, the Stowmarket turn (Brown sign)
Continue to Station Road and turn right, B1115
At Ilife Way (Brown sign) turn left
Public car park opposite the supermarket with reduction in charge for MEAL visitors at Tourist Information Centre

Adnams' pub:

Gladstone Arms Combs Ford, Stowmarket   01449 612339

Breckland and Grimes Graves

Spanning 370 square miles across south-west Norfolk and north-west Suffolk, this huge area stretches from the Fens in the west to the clay arable land that forms most of Suffolk.

It was given its name in the nineteenth century: 'breck' means a tract of heathland that was broken up for cultivation for a period, then allowed to return to the wild. Now popularly known as 'The Brecks', the open heath with sheep walks and rabbit warrens has been overshadowed by the vast areas of conifers planted by the Forestry Commission since 1922. Bracken grows everywhere.

This strange land lying between Bury St Edmunds in Suffolk and Thetford in Norfolk has a low rainfall, making it the driest region in Britain. The underlying chalk is covered by a layer of sand which suffers from serious 'blowing' that can uproot crops if they are not well-established.

Had it not been for the large flocks of sheep that grazed in the Brecks, the hungry soil would have had no chance of producing food for humans or animals. But it was rabbits that provided food and employment in the many warrens that existed in past times. The Brecks are thinly populated. Most of the villages are close to river valleys and the only towns on the Suffolk side of the border are Brandon, Mildenhall and Lakenheath.

A good place to start an exploration in the Brecks is at the Brandon Heritage Centre, where the main displays deal with rabbit farming, the use of their fur for hat making and flint mining. The replica of flint 'knapping' is exceptionally good. Close by, just across the Norfolk border is the site known as Grimes Graves, in the care of English Heritage. It takes its name from Anglo-Saxon times, when the curious 'moonscape' of the abandoned prehistoric flint mines was attributed to their god Grim.

Incredibly, 433 mine shafts have been identified and there may be many more buried under sand blows, all dug between 3000 BC and 2000 BC.

What makes Grimes Graves special is that it is the only flint mine in the country open to visitors. A visitor centre issues tickets for the ladderway access close by and has plenty of information material.

Flint is an extraordinarily hard rock which can be 'knapped', or separated into flakes with sharp edges that were highly valued by prehistoric men for making into tools and weapons. The flintlock gun used for so long by British and other armies was dependent on supplies of flints: Wellington certainly was at Waterloo. By 1813 Brandon was supplying over 1 million

Flint 'knapping' was a craft unique to the area and the tools for that craft are well displayed.

flints per month from local pits on Lingheath; it was not for nothing that the Brecks acquired the title 'The flint capital of Britain!'

The Neolithic miners used antler picks to excavate the flint nodules, working at various levels down the shafts; galleries were cut wherever the flints were of sufficient quantity. It is thought that baskets of flint nodules were raised to the surface up primitive ladders to platforms built at intervals in the shafts, which were up to 40ft deep.

Visitors at Grimes Graves use a security ladder to go down to look at the galleries under the supervision of an attendant: there are many finds on display and on the surface a wide range of animals and birds can be seen. A walk towards the trees on the edge of the site round the old mine shafts will show examples of flowering plants that enjoy chalk soils, such as purple wild thyme as well as acid soil-loving woodsage. Both types of soil are here, making the outdoor exploration as fascinating as going down the mine shaft.

The Brecks include Thetford Forest, the largest lowland pine forest in Britain, designated a Forest Park in 1990. Brandon itself has a country Park with way-marked walks, a tree and history trail and a splendid visitor centre with restaurant.

High Lodge Forest Centre is just south east of Brandon, from which visitors can walk, cycle, or ride the ancient trackways and bridleways; the variety of wild life is extraordinary, from red deer to the tiny goldcrest among the many birds. The Ling gunflint pits are here, also warrens where rabbits were farmed.

The ancient heaths have their own fascination, are ideal for exploring and have their own special wildlife that includes the rare stone curlew. There are, too, the isolated meres whose water levels suddenly and mysteriously vary.

Directions:

Brandon Heritage Centre:
A11 to Elveden, then B1106 into Brandon
Follow Thetford signs, B1107 and turn into George Street (one way), Centre opposite the Fire Station.

Grimes Graves:

Off A1065 Swaffham Road just over Norfolk border
High Lodge Forest Centre:
Off B1107 Brandon - Thetford Road

Adnams' pub:

Castle Inn   Castle street, Cambridge   01223 353194

Leiston

The Long Shop Museum

The founder of the company that brought Leiston fame was Richard Garrett who arrived from Woodbridge in 1778 to run a forge manufacturing sickles and scythes. His son followed him and in his time agricultural appliances such as threshing machines developed and by 1826 Richard Garrett III was head of a forward-looking company producing a wide range of machinery including horse power threshing machines, ploughs and seed drills.

Successive generations of the Garretts took over the company, which rapidly became the major employer in Leiston. No reminder was needed, but both town and countryside were told when work began and finished by the steam signal, the Leiston 'Bull'.

Always 'ahead of the game', Richard Garrett & Son Ltd, as the company became, exhibited at the Great Exhibition in 1861 and brought the railway to Leiston. Products at the turn of the century included locomotives, steam tractors and steam rollers: a second works site was developed next to the railway station, where a huge gantry handled heavy equipment to be moved by rail. In order to transport goods from the town works to the station a tramway was built, first using horse power and later by a well-loved steam loco. called 'Sirapite', now under restoration. During both World Wars production turned to military needs.

Garretts made one of the first attempts in the country to design an assembly line for portable steam engines. Called the Long Shop and dating from 1853, it successfully dealt with large numbers of repeat orders; over 15,000 of these were made, bringing the company international recognition. By the 1970s there was overseas financial control and in 1980 Garretts had to cease production.

The Works site has become a popular visit, becoming known as the Long Shop Museum. There was extensive restoration and the development of an exhibition gallery once occupied by fitters' benches with an overhead crane.

The Long Shop

In the former central erecting bay that occupied the full length of the building are examples of the products for which Garretts became famous: a threshing machine, (the predecessor of the combine harvester), a portable steam engine, a road roller and a traction engine.

Other buildings, including a tally house, office, water tower block and workshops have been restored: the site has become the High Green conservation area and the buildings have been listed. The Richard Garrett Hall displays early agricultural products of the company such as seed drills and a chaff cutter; horse power was needed for many of these early machines and led to the company's production of steam power and steam engines.

Details:

The Drawing Office and Works Office are open to view; interestingly, facing the Reception and Shop across the entrance is the former Works House and Head Office
Car Parking is at the rear of the Long Shop

Directions:

A12 to Saxmundham, then
B1119 to crossroads and lights at Leiston
Forward into Main Street
Long Shop Museum 100 yards on right

Adnams' pubs:

| Engineers Arms | Opposite Long Shop Museum, Leiston | 01728 830660 |
| Eels Foot | Leiston Road, Eastbridge | 01728 830154 (Accomm) |

Leiston Abbey

Although the ruins of the abbey of the Blessed Virgin Mary are within sight of the busy B1122 road from Leiston to Yoxford, it was not always so. The original site was on the marshland now part of the RSPB Nature Reserve at Minsmere. The danger of flooding forced the Praemonstratensian canons to seek permission to rebuild elsewhere and the 'new' abbey was built a mile or so north of Leiston, close to the turning to Eastbridge.

The date for the present ruins is late fourteenth century, although some older stone was used, taken from the original, abandoned building. In 1382 serious damage was caused by a fire which required a second rebuilding. Following the Dissolution of the Monasteries, the abbey lost much of its stone, but its layout remains clear. An unusual feature is the house built into the west end of the church and used today as a music school; the Great Barn facing the public car park is in excellent condition.

A late addition was a Tudor brick gatehouse with octagonal turrets from which there is a good view across the cloister to the chapter house. From the south the refectory (or frater) with a large west window is the nearest and most substantial building; beyond the other ruins to the north is the church, 168ft long.

Directions:

A12 to Yoxford, then B1122 via Theberton
or
A12 to Saxmundham, then B1119 to crossroads and lights at Leiston
Turn left on to B1122 into Station Road, over former railway crossing
Turn left at brown sign for abbey

Adnams' pubs:

Engineers Arms	Main Street, Leiston	01728 830660
Eels Foot	Leiston Road, Eastbridge	01728 830154

Sutton Hoo: Anglo Saxon Burial Ground of Kings

It was Mrs Edith Pretty, owner of the Sutton Hoo estate across the River Deben from Woodbridge in the 1930s, who engaged Basil Brown, a local archaeologist to examine the strange hummocks on the fields near her house. They were known to be burial mounds or barrows and had been attacked by grave robbers over the centuries; the atmosphere round the

The Leiston Abbey ruins are open to view just out of town, having moved from the Minsmere marshes when threatened by floods.

barrows affected Mrs Pretty and she determined to find out if anything was still to be learned from them.

Little did they know that they were to make one of the greatest archaeological discoveries ever made in Britain: Basil Brown found under what is known as Mound 1, a ship decayed to black powder in the sandy soil, the lines of the hull marked by rows of corroded rivets. It became clear that this was a royal burial mound containing a ship 27m long serving as a coffin and a means of travel into another world.

Together with the dead man, by 1939 reduced to a chemical trace in the soil, were his belongings, even the remains of clothing and leather items in a small enclosure: in pride of place were his sword and belt, helmet and shield. Spearheads were included for the use of the dead warrior. Of the decorative items were gold buckles and clasps, also drinking vessels for his journey, jewelled and chased with delicate interlaced patterns not seen before in Anglo Saxon work of the pre-Christian period.

As to the person whose burial ship this was, it is thought to have been Raedwald, King of East Anglia who died about AD 625. Why this grave was not robbed like the rest is a mystery: one theory is that the robbers' shaft into the barrow began to collapse and it was abandoned in panic.

Much has been learned from the total of twenty burial mounds and, fortunately, The National Trust, which manages the site, has put together a wonderful exhibition of the finds (mostly reproductions) and a spectacular recreation of the ship burial chamber and its treasures.

Wonder at the helmet, watch the video and walk to the burial ground, 500 metres away. There are guided walks lasting 1¼ hours which can be booked at the reception desk, or you can follow the excellent illustrated map. The route passes round the whole of the burial site and a viewing platform provides an overall impression as well as a fine photographic location. Mrs Pretty's house, not open to the public, is close to the Rabbit Field and beyond to the west is the River Deben with good views of Woodbridge.

Like all National Trust sites, Sutton Hoo has everything visitors might need: electric buggies, wheelchairs and hearing loops – all in addition to the video programme and a shop. The restaurant serves hot food from 11.30 am. to 2.30 pm. and offers a refreshment service during the site's opening hours. Allow plenty of time for Sutton Hoo: it may not be far from Woodbridge, but once there, visitors stay and there are countryside walks in addition to those to see the burial ground.

A circular walk reveals the cluster of graves and a brilliant recreation of the burial ship on display.

Directions:

From A12 follow Sutton Hoo signs on A1152
or
From Woodbridge B1438 to Melton
In both cases take the Wilford Bridge road at the crossroads
Cross the railway line and Wilford Bridge
At the roundabout fork right on B1083: Sutton Hoo car park on right

Adnams' pubs:

Kings Head	17 Market Hill, Woodbridge	01394 387750
Cherry Tree	73 Cumberland Street, Woodbridge	01394 382513 (Accomm)
Black Tiles	Black Tiles Lane, Martlesham	01473 624038

Easton Farm Park

May 2007 was a special month at the Farm Park; their Suffolk Punch Easton Star produced a foal, named Mary. Chesnut (the correct spelling for the breed) like all Punches, Mary had lovely eyes, a gorgeous skin and her legs were what any girl dreams of. While Easton Star would feed quietly in the middle of the paddock, Mary would lap up all the admiration of visitors at the fence. Now she is growing, of course.

While Easton is the ideal place to go to see a working farm with its machinery, tools, vehicles old and new and even a forge it is the animals that draw the crowds and command attention. Who could resist the nursery with newly hatched (and hatching) chicks, or a sow with her piglets?

Each day has an activity programme so that visitors can see and share the feeding of stock and there are pony and cart rides. Learn how to make corn dollies and herd the goats. In the summer of 2007 pygmy goats were on show and even for sale.

Easton Farm Park's animals attract crowds of visitors, especially their group of Suffolk Punches. Here are Rose, Mollie and Major.

'Where are the other Suffolk Punches?' I asked. 'Across the river' they said. It was not far, just over the little bridge beyond the Victorian Dairy. Do not miss the dairy on any account. I was on my own: there were three of them, Rose, Mollie and Major and we were friends immediately. What a day that was! These huge, gentle creatures are great workers and easy to handle when you have an understanding with them. You will find a history of the Suffolk Punch in the building close to the Victorian Dairy; at the end of the range of buildings by the diary is the Riverside café with seats under the cover or outside on the Deben River bank where there is always bird-life activity.

For a family holiday there are four star self-catering cottages on the farm; choose Bank Holiday at the end of May and you would be there for the sheep shearing.

The Farm park was once the Home Farm of the estate of the Duke of Hamilton, whose house was in the village, although no longer. What does remain is the crinkle-crankle wall that surrounded the grounds; not all of it, sadly, any more. Huge lengths of it do still stand, enough for a fair claim that it was (and is) the longest in East Anglia, perhaps in the world.

It is only a short walk form the Farm Park to the crossroads and must be seen. Take your camera.

Directions:

Easton Farm Park: A12 to Wickham Market
At the village roundabout take B1078 west
Fork right at the end of village at Easton sign
Cross bridge, pass church and crinkle-crankle wall
At crossroads follow sign to Farm Park

Adnams' pubs:

Kings Head	17 Market Hill, Woodbridge	01394 387750
Cherry Tree	73 Cumberland Street, Woodbridge	01394 382513 (Accomm)

Carlton Colville, Lowestoft – The East Anglia Transport Museum

They make the bold claim at Carlton Colville that it is the only place in the British Isles where you can ride on all the principal forms of public transport from the early part of the twentieth century. So it really is, as they say, a trip back in time. If you like free rides it is the right place to be!

The wide range of preserved vehicles – more than most collections – is still having additions, although limited covered accommodation means that only items of historic interest are likely to be accepted.

Now fully registered and having charitable status, the museum was officially opened in 1972, ten years after the body of a former Lowestoft tram was rescued from a country garden where it was in use as a summer house. Three years later, on a meadow provided by the Society's founder chairman, the society was formed to acquire and preserve public service vehicles from the past.

Today, supported by volunteers, restoring, maintaining and operating the fleet of vehicles, running the depots, offices, workshops, refreshment facilities and toilets, it is a thriving organisation.

Since the whole purpose is to illustrate movement, there are roads, tram tracks, power supplies for trams and trolley buses, even the rails for the East Suffolk Light Railway, which has a platform on Chapel Road Railway Station.

Finance is provided by entrance fees, also donations and subscriptions from members of the museum. No grants of any kind are received; since great emphasis is placed on the museum's educational role, it seems that an opportunity to support the museum is being missed.

Once through the entrance, passengers board the vehicles: tram, trolley bus or bus at the Chapel Road turning circle. Across to the right is the East Suffolk Light Railway.

Oulton Broad's East Anglian Transport Museum has the great attraction of providing free rides on its range of transport systems.

All the road vehicles pass through Tramway Avenue beyond the tram and bus depots, a park and picnic area, the trolley bus depot, post office and shops. The circular journeys through the built-up, then wooded areas are full of interest; street furniture such as a 1921 telephone kiosk, a war-time Anderson shelter and an elderly post box are reminders of earlier transport days.

There are outdoor displays of steam rollers and roadmen's living vans; under cover is a car showroom – vintage of course. As to the transport fleet, some are famous and have a long, distinguished pedigree, like *Blackpool* 159, an early covered tram, or *London* 260 trolley bus built for use in London in 1936. This looks up to date even now.

Lowestoft was well known for the town's Eastern Coach Works, which built buses for many authorities, including Eastern Counties. Examples of these with bodies built there for Lowestoft Corporation and Eastern Counties go back as far as 1947.

The East Suffolk Light Railway 2ft gauge line was opened in 1973 and the train goes to the 'country' terminus at Woodside and back with points there to allow the engine to run round the train for the return journey. There are four diesel locos donated by quarries and public utilities, one carriage having been built at the Museum on a running frame, also a brake van adapted to take wheelchairs.

Some of the track was once part of the Southwold Railway at Halesworth and, unmissable close to Chapel Road Station is the only surviving item of rolling stock from the Southwold Railway, closed in 1929- a renovated luggage van built in 1885.

Such are the numbers visiting the museum and the increasing range of things to see and do that plans are under way for a extension to the Terminus Tea Room; three areas have been already been set aside for picnics. Parking is free.

Directions:

Carlton Colville:
A12 to Lowestoft
Turn to Oulton Broad A1117
Possible delays at Oulton Broad North Station

Museum:

Chapel Road off A146 Beccles Road
Sign at roundabout

Adnams' pubs:

Butchers Arms	London Road, Beccles	01502 712243
Five Bells	Southwold Road, Wrentham	01502 675249 (Accomm)
Horse & Groom	London Road, Wrentham	01502 675279

Flixton, Bungay, Norfolk & Suffolk Aviation Museum

It was in the 1970s that the idea of an aviation collection was born. Little did the group of local enthusiasts expect that in the first year over 5,000 visitors would go to Flixton and the Nissen hut that housed the aviation collection.

Former airfields were considered for a new, larger home, then suddenly help came from Flixton itself: the then landlord of the village pub offered two meadows and a barn next to the pub for the society's use. Since then the hard work and dedication of the volunteers involved have made it possible to buy an additional seven acres of land to allow for expansion.

Hangars and other buildings have been erected as funds were raised to replace the small indoor space provided by the barn so there is now an indoor and outdoor collection of more than fifty aircraft of all ages and types as well as a huge exhibition of finds of all kinds. One of the earliest from the Second World War is an Avro Anson, restored from a sad decline to the greatest pleasure of the author whose first flight 'in anger' in that war was on one of them.

In spite of the fact that the museum, now a registered charity, has never charged for admission – and parking is free – it has grown and flourished. Visitors are generous with their contributions, the shop earns a valuable income, there is regular fund-raising, there are donations from individuals and charities and support from Waveney District Council. Donations of memorabilia come in all the time, some so large and costly to bring to the site that they cannot be accepted.

Perhaps the sight of a Bloodhound Surface to Air Missile is one of the more unexpected outdoor exhibits; equally unexpected is the engine of a wartime V2 rocket, some forty of which were targeted on Norwich from Holland in the closing stages of the war.

As the museum developed several individual exhibitions and memorials were set up on the site, notably on behalf of the 446 Bomb Group of the United States Air Force.

The 446th was based at Flixton airfield from 1943 to 1945 and has its own exhibition and a memorial to those who died or served with the Group.

Similarly there are museums for RAF Bomber Command, the Royal Observer Corps, Air-Sea Rescue and Coastal Command: 'The sea shall not have them'. A statue of an RAF Sergeant Pilot of 1940 was unveiled in 2000 to mark the 60th anniversary of the Battle of Britain.

Flixton has so many aircraft to display that how best to show them must have presented an acute problem. Wisely it was decided to go for maximum impact and it was achieved with a Gloster Javelin just inside the entrance gate; close by is another attack aircraft, a French Mystere, both shown in immaculate condition and squadron-ready. The museum guide *The Flixton Story* lists all the items on display.

Such is the wealth of photographs, maps, documents and artifacts of all kinds that special rooms house them. Storage is a problem, but the archives are now very valuable and are called upon for research programmes nationally.

Directions:

A14 and A140 north
At Scole roundabout turn on to A143 east towards Bungay
At Homersfield turn on to B1062 (see sign)
or
A12 north, over railway crossing at Darsham Station
In about one mile turn left on A144 for Halesworth and Bungay
Entering Bungay turn left on B1062 for Flixton

Adnams' pubs:

Fleece Inn   St Mary's Street, Bungay   01986 892192

The Buck at Flixton is next door to the Museum and Flixton Post Office next door to the Buck
has customarily offered bed and breakfast.

West Stow Anglo-Saxon Village

As an illustration of 'the way we were', West Stow is unbeatable, especially as the timescale is so
great. The finds there and the reconstruction of the village reflect the days of tribal pressure in
Northern Europe that created a migration of land-hungry people from Northern Germany
and Denmark.

In Britain Roman rule was collapsing in 410-420 and the open estuaries on the east coast must
have presented an opportunity for new settlers too good to miss. Settlements along the Orwell
and Gipping beyond Ipswich showed the way; West Stow along the River Lark was little further.

What has allowed so much of the early Anglo-Saxon period to survive undisturbed at West
Stow is the large quantity of wind-blown sand typical of the landscape there that covered
the area since medieval times. The soil itself had no acid content, so bones, metal objects and
domestic items have been preserved until now.

The West Stow Anglo-Saxon village near Bury St Edmunds has been re-created exactly as it once
appeared.

Had it not been for the discovery of skeletons and urns in what was clearly an ancient cemetery at West Stow by men excavating for gravel in 1847, there might have been little interest in the site. But afterwards local historians and collectors began to investigate and made more valuable finds. West Stow was explored from 1957 for a number of years until in 1972 Bury St Edmunds Council agreed to support a reconstruction of the village and to gather together an exhibition of finds made there.

It was concluded that the buildings were of wood as this was the only material in common use and traditional skills would have developed in working with it; traditional also was the design of the homes and workshops built in settlement communities elsewhere.

Two types of buildings were found to have existed at West Stow, probably 'hall' houses serving as family or community accommodation and, round them, groups of smaller units mainly used as work places and for sleeping. Post holes show that the hall houses were some 30ft long with a door on one side and often at the end as well.

Evidence from burned houses suggest vertical planked walls, but whether there were floors is not known; roofs would certainly have been thatched using reeds or straw. Clay pads suggested that there were central hearths in the hall houses used for heating and cooking. Finds of animal bones and of seeds have given much information about the food eaten at West Stow, the cattle, sheep and pigs they kept – even the horses used as working animals.

The smaller buildings appear to be similarly constructed, but with a boarded floor over a pit about 13ft long that may well have been used for storage and allowed dry air to circulate. Finds of loom weights and bone needles confirm the vital work of weaving went on in these buildings; leatherworking and pottery were essential to life, also the making of tools and weapons for hunting and more evidence shows that these activities took place there.

Below the Visitor Centre at West Stow is an exhibition gallery of remarkable size and quality, adding another dimension to the understanding of West Stow. It includes a farming and hunting section with wood, bone and metal finds; there are also displays of tools, pottery, decorative work and even an Anglo-Saxon fashion show!

It should be remembered that the Anglo-Saxon village is just part of the West Stow Country Park; paths and trails open up the whole area, well way-marked for walkers. Follow the path from

Research has revealed that an Anglo-Saxon way of life existed here, and the interior of the dwellings at West Stow illustrate this well.

the visitor centre for the reconstructed village and it will be clear how its territory stretched from the river meadows and arable area upwards to drier ground where sheep would have grazed.

The visitor centre and entrance desk is of course, the first calling point (there is an extensive car park and a restaurant) to pick up a handout map 'West Stow Country Park: paths and trails'. From the extensive book store I strongly recommend *Understand West Stow*, published by Jarrolds which is well written and illustrated with photographs, diagrams and maps.

Directions:

West Stow: From A14 junction 42 B1106 to Fornham All Saints
Turn left on A1101 through Hengrave, Flempton and Lackford, then right at sign for the village.

Adnams' pubs:

Gladstone Arms	Combs Ford, Stowmarket	01449 612339
Castle Inn	Castle Street, Cambridge	01223 353194

Framlingham

The town's historical importance came from the castle built by the Bigods. None of the other fortresses in East Anglia was bigger than that at Framlingham and none was like it, being the first in the whole of the country not to have a traditional keep.

Without doubt the whole of the country round Framlingham was dependent on and obedient to the lord of the castle, so the town became a focus of life and work. A market there served the neighbourhood, roads led to it and – much later – a railway.

The earliest part of the town to develop was in and around the triangular Market Hill; traders brought their produce there and shops and inns were established. The so-called Guildhall, a row of eighteenth-century shops along one side of Market Hill is particularly attractive with the

Framlingham Castle, once a Howard stronghold, is best viewed across the mere, part of the water defences.

tower of St Michael's Church just behind. Opposite is the Crown pub, used in the old days as a coach stop; there were plenty of ale houses in Framlingham.

St Michael's Church is not only architecturally beautiful, but historically important as well, not least because of the monuments and tombs of the Howards. The most important is the tomb of Thomas Howard, 3rd Duke of Norfolk. The 96ft tower was built between 1483 and 1520 and is decorated with flushwork as is the clerestory.

The roof is superb, being supported by hammer beams, decorated and covered by vaulted coving as at St Peter Mancroft on the Market Place at Norwich. The chancel was extended in the sixteenth century to provide more space for monuments at least 100 years after the church was built.

In the west arch of the nave is the famous Thamar organ built for Pembroke College in 1674 and moved to the church in 1708. This came about following Sir Robert Hitcham's purchase of the castle and his presentation of it to Pembroke College. Behind the high altar is the reredos and the mystical painting, *The Glory*, dated 1700.

The Hitcham Almshouses of 1674, one of Sir Robert's many bequests are in New Road, across the bridge below Market Hill and to the right; easily recognised, they are single storeyed and have a central gable. Further along New Road is the classic view of the castle across the mere. It is well worth the walk to admire it.

Framlingham's many Georgian houses are too often concealed behind nineteenth-century frontages. Perhaps the best of the seventeenth century is the Ancient House in Albert Place. Its central doorway, hipped roof and oval pargetting either side of the central first-floor window are a real pleasure; look for it by the pedestrian crossing.

Framlingham has several maltings and flour mills; the latter have now gone, but one fascinating fragment of a former smock mill remains. The base of the mill has been thatched and converted into a handsome house; attached to it is a more modern wing. It is at the end of a curved drive leading off Station Road between Brook Lane and Victoria Mill Road, not far from Adnams' Railway Inn.

The round house, a former smock mill near the old railway station, is one of many houses of interest in Framlingham.

The Castle

The powerful stronghold at Framlingham was strengthened by ditches dug to protect the site; the Castle Mere was also created to form part of its defence using material from the ditch excavation to make a dam to hold back the water in the Mere.

Entrance to the castle is across the moat through a heavy gate once protected by a drawbridge and a portcullis. Above the gate is the Howard coat of arms, a reminder that after the Crown took over the castle from the Bigods in 1306, ownership passed to the Mowbrays, then through the female line to the Howards, Dukes of Norfolk. They, in their turn, lost the castle in Henry VIIIs reign; Edward VI gave it to Mary Tudor, his half sister. She was at Framlingham in 1533 and was proclaimed Queen there before marching to London to remove Lady Jane Grey from the throne of England.

There are fine views of the countryside, including the mere, from the castle walkways along the walls. It was the thirteen flanking towers along the massive wall that made Framlingham so strong; high up on the walkways looking rather grotesque, are huge decorated Tudor chimneys.

On the east side of the inner court, or bailey, are remains of the earliest Bigod buildings; a stone hall and a chapel. The west side's buildings once included a kitchen (a fireplace is visible there), a postern gate that gave access to a Prison Tower and a Poor House on the site of the Great Hall. This substantial and interesting building was added after the sale of the castle by the Howards to Sir Robert Hitcham in 1635. Sir Robert bequeathed it to Pembroke College on condition of the building of the Poor House on the site of the Great Hall. In 1913 the castle passed into public ownership.

Directions:

Framlingham: A12 to Saxmundham then B1119 via Rendham

The Poor House, erected within the castle in 1729, houses the information centre and shop.

or

A14 Junction 50 then tourist route A1120 to Saxtead Green (Note Mill)
B1119 east
In Framlingham take Church Street and Castle Street to the Castle
Car parking at castle

Adnams' pubs:

Railway Inn	Station Road, Framlingham	01728 723693
White Horse	Woodbridge Road, Badingham	01728 638280

Orford

Although there are several routes from the A12 to Orford, many people visit Snape Maltings on the way. Everything depends on your plans for exploring when you reach Orford and the time you have available.

Prominent as you approach Orford is the spectacular castle keep; the view of the castle from the riverbank which shows the church tower and the roofs of the town as well is one of the most attractive on this stretch of the coast.

As the long spit of the land opposite the harbour and known as Orfordness extended further and further south, the result of shingle deposits from tidal activity, so Orford found itself further from the sea. But long ago in 1165 when King Henry II ordered work to begin on building a castle (it was finished in 1172), the harbour faced the open sea and it is tempting to think that Orford Castle, was needed for coastal defence. Not so: at that time the king was facing rebellion from East Anglian barons with fortresses of their own and he could only maintain his authority if he had a visible sign of royal power – a castle.

Unlike the earlier rectangular castle keeps, Orford's central core was polygonal – the interior being cylindrical with walls 10ft thick. This made it easier to defend and more difficult to undermine. Three strong turrets rising higher than the main tower buttressed it, provided rooms at each level and stair access to them. Within the main tower were a basement and lower and upper halls.

Earthworks consisting of a series of ditches and ramparts strengthened the whole site; some of this has now disappeared. From the top of the keep are magnificent views of Orfordness, the sea and south down the river towards Shingle Street.

To the east of the Market Place is St Bartholomew's Church; only the remains of the original huge Norman chancel can be seen, with today's fourteenth-century church having been built in the Decorated style. The top of the tall west tower fell in 1830, but it is still powerful with large buttresses.

Although there is a good car park next to the quay, the walk there from the Market Place past the fisherman's cottages and a visit to the seventeenth-century Jolly Sailor (Adnams) are well worthwhile, so is the walk along the riverbank to Chantry Point.

Orford Marine Services offer river trips from the quay and there are also RSPB boat trips to Havergate Island. (see p. 131) The National Trust National Nature Reserve on the Ness can be visited by ferry only at weekends between April and October. Details from 01394 450057 and 01394 450900. Visitors follow a 5½ mile route which can be walked in total or in part. The reserve is an important location for breeding and passage birds as well as for costal flora and fauna.

As The National Trust Magazine puts it, Orford Ness is an unconventional nature reserve; there is a lack of interference by the trust with visitors which adds to the sense of wilderness, where wild life is quietly taking over.

The Ness was a secret military site from 1913 until the mid-1980s; bombing was researched, radar development and atomic weapons tested. Concrete bunkers, strange 'pagoda' type buildings and towers remain from these activities.

A walk along the river bank offers a fine view of the village, the castle and the parish church.

A view east from the castle ramparts shows how important Orford was for defence.

A good deal of Orford's past has a strange element: floods, secret wartime 'happenings', for example, and then there was the Orford Merman! At about the time of the building of the castle some fisherman are supposed to have netted a curious bearded creature like a man. He had no speech and lived on a diet of raw fish; eventually they took him back to the sea. He seemed not to want to leave Orford and he swam back; some time later, so the story goes, he did go back to the sea and disappeared forever. It is said that he was unhappy: as he could not speak, how did they know? *Orford: see details for Havergate Island.*

4

Market Towns and Historic Villages

Aldeburgh

There have been two Aldeburghs: a small, poor fishing and shipbuilding town in early times and a sophisticated, genteel, prosperous watering place today.

The wind and the waves have always been the great enemy, sweeping away the easterly part of the town and leaving the Moot Hall on Market Cross Place almost stranded on the seashore. At Slaughden Quay, once the fishing, shipbuilding and trading area south of the town, a narrow shingle spit is all that remains to protect the River Alde from the sea.

Life was hard in the old days: smuggling was common and wrecks took place with sad regularity. There was an acceptance of danger, even a willingness of crews to man lifeboats in impossible conditions. The name Cable is recorded with honour in the history of the various Aldeburgh lifeboats and the writing of George Crabbe is a record of the dark aspects of conditions in the town at the beginning of the nineteenth century.

His poems cover up none of the poverty and squalor he saw; of them all, *The Borough* dwelt on Aldeburgh itself and established his greatness with the character of Peter Grimes the fisherman. Byron called him 'Nature's sternest poet, yet the best'. Other names and great talents show how Aldeburgh's fascination brought to the town men who would make it famous. An unlikely visitor was Edward Fitzgerald from Woodbridge; he was another poet and translated the *Rubaiyat of Omar Khayam*. He said he was 'happiest going in my little boat round the coast to Aldbro''. He contended that the Aldeburgh sea spoke to him.

Aldeburgh needed the imagination and energy of the Victorians to become the sort of place it is today. Newson Garrett, a grandson of the founder of the engineering works at Leiston moved to Aldeburgh and set about the town's development, building and promoting the town as a seaside resort. The extension of the Old Reading Room to become the Jubilee Hall for Queen Victoria's Jubilee in 1867 and the building of Snape Maltings are examples of his work. His second daughter, Elizabeth Garrett Anderson became the first woman doctor and with her husband founded the hospital entirely for women in London bearing her name. In Aldeburgh in 1908 she became the first woman mayor in the country.

Most recent of all was the arrival of Benjamin Britten and Peter Pears. After a period in Canada they returned and in 1944 Britten began work on *Peter Grimes,* George Crabbe's character in *The Borough*. In 1948 the first Aldeburgh Festival was held, using the Jubilee Hall and local churches as venues. The great day came in 1967 when the Queen opened the Snape Maltings Concert Hall. Among the many honours Britten received were the Freedoms of Aldeburgh and of his home town, Lowestoft. He is buried at the church of St Peter and St Paul at Aldeburgh.

Exploring Aldeburgh should start at the Moot Hall, where there are hotels and good parking; it is timber framed, dates from 1520 to 1540 and has always served as the town hall. In early days markets were held at ground-floor level; today the building has a fine museum and still provides a council chamber.

Just opposite is the Mill Inn (Adnams, of course!), almost as old as the Moot Hall; its leaded windows have a fine view of the sea and no doubt could tell many stories of smuggling days.

The Moot Hall (Council Chamber) at Aldeburgh also serves as the town's museum.

Walking south offers a choice: Crabbe Street or High Street, which meet at Baggott's corner. Beyond, the street widens and there are parking spaces outside the shops, the former Suffolk Hotel and Tourist Information Centre.

An alternative route is along the Crag Path, past sea front houses; Aldeburgh, like Chillesford, near Orford stands on deposits of Coralline or Shelly Crag. The tower of Chillesford Church is built of it. On the beach itself is the Lifeboat Station and two lookouts, used as watch towers by competing pilot groups trying to secure navigation business from ships at sea making for the Thames. No longer!

Marking the end of the Crag Path at Fort Green is the Old Mill, once used for milling flour; it is now converted into flats. There is a car park here and the local bus turns round. Slaughden is across the road, where George Crabbe laboured, the River Alde only yards away, modern shipyards and the Yacht Club further along. The sea and river are only separated by the spit of land that continues for nearly ten miles to Shingle Street; along the way the Butley River joins the Aide which then changes to the Ore.

It is worth walking the extra distance to see the Martello Tower at close quarters. The most northerly and the largest of the towers built to defend the east coast from a possible Napoleonic invasion that at Aldeburgh was not completed until 1815 when the danger was long past. The tower design came from Torra della Mortella in Corsica where defences withstood bombardment in 1794; quatrefoil in shape, Aldeburgh's Martello Tower has massively thick walls, but its gun batteries and moat have gone. Today the Landmark Trust offers accommodation there for holidaymakers.

There is limited unauthorised parking along the narrow access road there, but it is a shame not to walk with so much river activity to see. The beach walk is tempting, but it is hard work and painful to the feet on the shingle; the road is a better alternative.

On the return the bend of the river shows where Slaughden used to be, although the buildings of this settlement were swept away; the wide river winds its way towards Snape. The Brudenell Hotel beyond Fort Green is the first major building on the south of Aldeburgh proper; continuing towards the High street look for Priors Hill Road and the cottages beyond it on the left. The best of them are near the Old Custom House, built around 1703, which became the home of George Crabbe's father, a collector of salt duties; George's birthplace was lost to the sea.

Aldeburgh has a fine example of an east-coast Martello Tower, built as a defence against Napoleon. You can rent it for your holiday.

Roads on the left lead steeply up the cliff to the 'other' Aldeburgh, where the affluent built their large houses, especially the incomers.

My preference is to go up the Town Steps, just beyond the post office and the Coop (there are seats by the upper steps which offer people like me a rest with a magnificent view over roofs and out to sea).

In addition to the annual Aldeburgh Festival there are regular musical events in the town and the cinema flourishes: it is a short distance along High Street towards the Moot Hall. The sixteenth-century church of St Peter and St Paul is on Church Hill, a turning on the left at the end of the High Street; its condition was poor in the nineteenth century and there was considerable restoration.

Directions:

Aldeburgh: A12 to Friday Street.
(Sixteen miles north of Ipswich)
Then right A1094 7 miles to Aldeburgh

Adnams' pubs:

Mill Inn	Market Cross, Aldeburgh	01728 452563
White Hart	High Street, Aldeburgh	01728 453205
Cross Keys	Crabbe Street, Aldeburgh	01728 452637 (Accomm)
Railway Inn	Leiston Road, Aldeburgh	01728 453864

Thorpeness

The two-mile journey from Aldeburgh north to Thorpeness is full of interest; it is beside the sea all the way on the right and on the left are Church Farm Marshes, acquired by the RSPB.

About halfway, standing on the shingle is the controversial sculpture by Maggi Hambling called Scallop. She wanted it to be a place where people could converse with the sea and listen; she remembers as a child holding a shell to her ear to listen and this was her tribute to Benjamin Britten. When you go, remember how important it is to walk completely round Scallop so that it can be seen from all angles – and to listen and converse with the sea.

Thorpeness was founded nearly a century ago by Glencairn Stuart Ogilvie as a holiday village where previously there had only been a collection of fishermen's cottages. He laid out roads lined with black and white weather-boarded houses in a neo-Tudor style round the Mere, a shallow freshwater lake for boating and fishing. Everything for families on holiday was planned: a hotel, a golf course, tennis courts, a pub (the Dolphin), a village shop, crafts, a bistro and a country club. Walking and bird watching are popular with summer residents: the RSPB North Warren and Aldringham Walks are close by.

On the skyline on the common are two well-loved landmarks; a post mill brought from neighbouring Aldringham and re-erected to pump a water supply and a water tower like nothing anywhere else, the House in the Clouds. The water tower is there all right, hidden underneath what appears to be an elevated house – originally a total fiction. In the end it was an opportunity too good to miss and was converted into a real residence. What a view!

The only real handicap to the continuing success of Thorpeness was the distance to and from the Halt on the branch railway line to Aldeburgh; the coming of the motor car changed everything and Thorpeness has never looked back.

Adnams' pubs: see Aldeburgh p. 78

Beccles

Only six miles downstream from Bungay, Beccles is a larger neighbour. There are only two route possibilities between them: the A143/146 (using the Bungay by-pass) or the B1062 on the Suffolk side of the Waveney.

Enlarged as a holiday attraction, the mere offers safe yet adventurous boating.

Thorpeness, only two miles north of Aldeburgh, was built as a holiday village, easily recognised by its 'House in the Clouds'.

The Quay, Yacht Station and Boatyards at Beccles have a leisure atmosphere that speaks of affluence. Much goes on there and the location of a Tourist Information Centre by the Quay is perhaps a reflection that Lowestoft is not far away and the river is navigable as far as this.

The influence of continental Europe is evident at Beccles just as it is at Lowestoft. Northgate which leads from the Old Market towards the Quay has some lovely examples of Dutch styles in the architecture of the larger houses. Lacking in building stone, Suffolk had to turn to brick when timbering became outdated and the early use of brick and pantiles in the Netherlands led to imports to east coast towns in the seventeenth century.

Beccles has pantiled roofs and houses of rich red brick with decorated gables which have a strong Dutch feeling. Early decorated gables were of the stepped variety sometimes called 'crow steps' and Beccles has a beautiful example at Roos Hall on the Bungay Road B1062. Built in 1593, its steeply pitched roof has four-storeyed gable ends with steps; at the corners of the building are buttresses which climb up level with the point of the gable and have decorated pinnacles. Stepped gables went out of fashion and were replaced by curved gables; these became popular in eastern England and over fifty of these have been identified in Suffolk alone.

Equally fascinating are the 'crinkle–crankle', ribbon, or serpentine walls first developed in the Netherlands to shelter and encourage climbing fruit trees, apples, pears, peaches and apricots; again, many are listed in Suffolk. Look for examples near Beccles at Ringsfield, Worlingham and Geldeston.

Surprisingly, the narrow alleyways leading from Northgate down to the river have the same 'scores', as those at Lowestoft from the High street to the waterside area. Central Beccles is only some 50ft above the riverbank, yet the slope down is sometimes referred to as 'the cliff'; any substantial rise or fall in the ground is, after all, a complete contrast to the marshes around town.

It was the danger of building a west tower to St Michael's Church on the edge of 'the cliff' that caused it to be built separated from the rest. St Michael's is in a superb position and can be seen from far away. The body of the church goes back to 1369, but the interior was destroyed by fire in 1586; its restoration left it less impressive than the tower, built in about 1455. By then river traffic was increasing and wool was being exported; Beccles was a prosperous town and wealth went into the tower which is stone-fronted. There are crocketed

Roos Hall, just out of town on the
Suffolk route to Bungay, is the finest
gabled house in the district.

Beccles is one of the larger market
towns. Overlooking the Waveney is the
impressive St Michael's Church.

Leman House, Beccles' museum, is located in the old Sir John Leman School building of 1631.

pinnacles, a crested parapet and heads over the doorway. Within is a vaulted ceiling with bosses; this is the gem of Beccles.

Another interesting church is the Roman Catholic St Benet's in St Mary's Road; built in the Romanesque style in 1889 it was planned to be part of a Benedictine priory. This end of St Mary's Road, a delightful part of Beccles leads into B1062, the Bungay Road for anyone interested in Roos Hall. Also from here, Ringsfield Road leads out of town; if you want to see the crinkle-crankle wall, turn at Ringsfield Church and you will find it on the far side of the churchyard. The other example at Worlingham is off the Lowestoft Road, a feature of a modern housing development in a road called 'The Bridles'.

The Lowestoft–Norwich Road A146 now, fortunately, bypasses Beccles; many visitors approach the town from the roundabout on the A145. On the left behind a superstore and industrial buildings is Beccles Marshes, given to the town by Queen Elizabeth I as the town sign shows. The Marsh Trail gives an opportunity to see the wildlife that flourishes there.

Turn right at Station road for the town centre and car parks. When Beccles was a busy railway junction it had a main route from London to Haddiscoe and Yarmouth Southtown and two branch lines: the Waveney Valley service to Bungay and Tivetshall and a well-used route to Oulton Broad and Lowestoft. Closures have meant that Beccles is now only a stop for trains on the Lowestoft to Ipswich route, an unimpressive service with connections at Ipswich for London. The East Suffolk Travellers' Association is a forceful campaigner for improvements of all kinds, both for rail and bus.

There is a pattern of place names between Beccles and Bungay: Gillingham, Ditchingham and Mettingham. Separate from that group is Geldeston on the Norfolk bank of the river where there is a lock and the end of the river navigation for craft from Beccles. A 'cut' gives access from the Waveney to the village, a not unusual feature, as local industry in places like Geldeston would have been dependent on the river for transportation. In the past fuel supplies would have come in and local products such as malt would have been shipped out that way.

Geldeston has a nice little pub (see below) built in the early eighteenth century, but the village remains much as it has always been. The church of St Michael has a round tower and the Old House has a well preserved crinkle-crankle wall sheltering its garden from the public highway.

Adnams' pubs:

Butchers Arms	London Road, Beccles	01502 712243
Wherry Inn	7 The Street, Geldeston	01508 518371

Bungay

Few Suffolk towns have so much to show in 'little compass' as Bungay; the town trail which was designed for the convenience of visitors suggests about 1½ hours to complete the walk at a normal pace. Outside the trail itself is Outney Common, enclosed within a great loop of the River Waveney: make time for a walk through the golden gorse along the surfaced paths. Take Earsham Street (find out the right pronunciation too!) past the post office, turn into Outney Road and cross the footbridge on to the common. Below is the bypass, built along the route of the former Beccles-Bungay-Tivetshall railway line.

Visitors to Bungay are often advised to start their exploration at the Butter Cross by the road junction at the centre of the town. Columned and domed, it was built in 1689 to replace its predecessor destroyed in the Great Fire of Bungay the previous year. Markets are still held there on Thursdays: readers of 'a certain age' will recall the trader who for years thanked his customers with a catch phrase 'I appreciate you very much'.

Even more prominent than the Butter Cross is the tower of St Mary's Church nearby; with four tall pinnacles and flushwork on the buttresses; much of the church was rebuilt following the fire of 1688. At the east end of the nave are the ruins of the Benedictine Priory of St Mary, including the nuns' choir. St Mary's is now redundant and is in the care of the Churches' Conservation Trust.

The legend of the Black Dog is strong in Bungay, as it is in Blythburgh (see p. 111) in August 1577 it is said to have appeared at St Mary's, killing two of the congregation and burning others.

With the increasing popularity of cruising, the Yacht Station and boat yards are always busy.

St Mary's, with a prominent tower, was a priory church. Ruins of the priory buildings remain at the east end.

Just south along St Mary's Street is the Roman Catholic church of St Edmund carrying a sculpture of his martyrdom. The oldest church in Bungay is Holy Trinity, a few yards to the south of the priory ruins. Its round tower with herringbone masonry is Saxon and fortunately it escaped serious damage in the Great Fire; its restored chancel is nineteenth century.

Across St Mary's Street by the side of the Swan Inn is a lane that leads to Bungay Castle, built by Roger Bigod in 1294 to replace an earlier fortress built by Hugh Bigod. The Bigods were lords of the manor at Framlingham, too, and built a great castle there. (see p. 73)

At Bungay little remains other than two great towers protecting the now disappeared drawbridge; also the foundations of the keep that was tunnelled when the castle was about to be undermined and destroyed on the orders of the king. A Castle Visitors' Centre has been set up with assistance from matched European funding; refreshments there can be recommended and there is an information section well-supplied with tourist material. Close by to the right of the centre are Castle Hills, part of the defensive earthworks built to protect the town.

Bungay has always been dependent on the river for its business and its trade: like all the towns and villages on the Waveney, it had its staithe, or quayside. Until the seventeenth century sizable craft could only go upstream as far as Beccles: when the trading wherries began to reach Bungay is not clear. There were shallows and blockages and until large enough locks had been constructed to accommodate the wherries Bungay's development was slow.

Wherries were the trading workhorses of the rivers and the Broads. Designed to be totally fit for their purpose, they drew no more than 4ft, yet could carry loads of up to 40tons. Totally dependent on the wind; their tall black sails and fore-and-aft rig caught every trace of wind; their ability to manoeuvre was extraordinary. The mast could be lowered quickly to allow a wherry to 'shoot' a bridge; balanced by 1-ton counterweight it could be brought up again without losing way. With a crew of two they could carry timber, coal, roadstone and chalk for cement from coasting vessels; outward went all the products of the countryside.

The round-towered Holy Trinity Church escaped the great fire that destroyed most of the town.

Bungay is only a few miles upstream from Beccles. In a huge loop of the Waveney it is guarded by the ruins of Bigod's Castle.

A traditional wherry, now sadly gone as a trading vessel.

So important were the wherries that millers, corn merchants and maltsters had their own; by the end of the nineteenth century there were some 200 black-sailed wherries on the rivers and Broads. The best known of all the wherry builders was William Brighton who started work at Bungay in 1861; after moving to Norwich he ended his career at Oulton Broad. His last and most famous wherry was *Albion*, built for Walkers' maltsters and merchants of Bungay in 1898 on the bank of Lake Lothing.

There are no more trading wherries at Bungay staithe but for many years they had busy lives. The most remarkable was Brighton's *Albion*; she sank in 1929, but was raised and went on working until the Second World War. Finally working as a lighter at Colman's she was rescued and restored by the Norfolk Wherry Trust in 1949.

Rivers like the Waveney were valuable as sources of water for malting and for transporting products to markets. An unusual agricultural development at Bungay was the commercial production of willow trees for making cricket bats. The moist river meadows are particularly suitable for plantation growing. Edgar Watts started in business in a small way in 1910; today trading as 'Three Willows Garden Centre', Peter Watts grows willows on various rented meadows including land at the Flixton Aviation Museum. As Peter says, the company's production is small in the wider scheme of things; 10,000 bats per year is unusual for a family business and significant for Bungay.

Malting was once big business locally, but concentration of production elsewhere led to the closure of the big Wainford Maltings which in 2008 was being converted into residential apartments.

Surprising to many visitors is the existence of the large Clay's printing company, nationally known as the Chaucer Press. Its life began in 1794 with the establishment of a small printing business in London by Richard Morris. In 1808 he was joined by John Childs in Bungay who brought other members of his family into the company; when John's son died the business was taken over by Richard Clay.

Three features led to the company's continued growth and success: the concentration of products at Bungay, the coming of the railway and a decision to specialise in paperback production such as Penguin Books. Although most of the employees are from Bungay increasing numbers come from Beccles, Norwich and elsewhere.

Adnams' pubs:

| Fleece Inn | St Mary's Street, Bungay | 01986 892192 |
| Butchers Arms | London Road, Beccles | 01502 712243 |

Snape and the Maltings

Just five miles of heath and marshland separate Snape and Aldeburgh. The River Alde is a visible link; it is tidal as far as Snape, which is the limit of navigation inland and at high tide sailing barges up to 100 tons could berth at the quay by the Maltings. Modern vessels of much greater weight are able to do so today.

The Aldeburgh Festival of Music and the Arts which was established in 1948 as a result of the inspiration of Benjamin Britten and Peter Pears became so popular that by the 1960s the Aldeburgh Jubilee Hall and local churches became inadequate for growing audience numbers. In 1967 the festival was held for the first time at the Snape Maltings Concert Hall; such is the power of coincidence that the Maltings had ceased to operate as a business just as the Festival was looking for a suitable home. The Maltings has exceptional acoustics and proved to be exactly what the Festival needed.

Snape begins at a crossroads on the A1094 Aldeburgh Road where the parish church of St John the Baptist stands well apart from the rest of the village that gives its name to the Maltings.

As the Maltings lie south of the river bridge, it is really in the parish of Tunstall on the road to Orford and Woodbridge. This has always been rich agricultural country and Snape attracted merchants and businessmen who could arrange river-borne cargoes of corn to go out and coal and building materials to be brought in.

The future of Snape Maltings was decided in 1841 when Newson Garrett, a vigorous and imaginative businessman took over a merchant's firm, determined to develop and expand it. This he did, increasing the outward cargoes of barley and, true to his Victorian character, looked

Snape Maltings is now an important visitor attraction, currently being extended. It is famous for its music; the concert hall was the brainchild of Benjamin Britten and Peter Pears.

for new ideas. He moved into malting, realising that it would be good business to supply breweries with malt, allowing them to concentrate on brewing. Newson's insistence on a branch railway line being built to Snape and a rail network being laid throughout the maltings shows how ready he was to adopt profitable changes.

The Garretts were talented: Newson's elder brother was the driving force that made Garrett's engineering works at Leiston so successful (see below). Newson had a large house built at Aldeburgh, where he became an important citizen, was mayor three times and brought up his family (six girls and four boys). His second daughter Elizabeth became famous as Elizabeth Garrett Anderson, the first woman to qualify in Britain as a doctor.

The First World War brought many problems including that of management of the company and Newson Garrett & Son was merged with Swonnell & Son; a representative of the Garrett family continued to serve the merged companies until they closed in 1965. For some years the Music Festival took place alongside the loading and unloading of cargoes at the quay, but by the 1980s all industrial work at the Maltings had ceased. The whole site became a conservation area and shops and galleries were opened; painting and craft courses began, also training courses for the world's young professional musicians. The Granary Tea Shop is open throughout the day and next to the Maltings is the Plough & Sail with a bar and a modern restaurant.

Out of doors energetic visitors can follow marked walks along the Alde estuary and on the first Saturday of each month there is an RSPB guided walk. For those who love to be on the water, river trips are available as tide times allow.

Directions:

Snape Maltings: A12 to Friday Street south of Saxmundham
Take A1094 (Aldeburgh Road) to Snape Church

Leiston's former Garrett's engineering works, 'the Long Shop', has been preserved with agricultural machinery once produced there.

Garrett's traction engines enabled power to be provided on farms in Suffolk and over a worldwide market.

Turn right through the village and cross bridge
Ample parking behind the Maltings

Adnams' pubs:

Crown Inn	Bridge Road, Snape	01728 688324 (Accomm)
Golden Key	Priory Road, Snape	01728 688510 (Accomm)

Wattisfield and Henry Watson's Potteries

(*With acknowledgement to Wattisfield Parish Council*)

A major route connecting the A14 and the huge sugar factory standing alongside it at Bury St Edmunds with business and holiday destinations in Suffolk and Norfolk is bound to attract considerable traffic, especially in the summer and the sugar beet season.

So it is that a steady flow of vehicles passes relatively slowly through Wattisfield and other villages on the A143. One village may have an unusual pub sign, another a fine round tower church: Wattisfield is different with its sign 'Henry Watson's Potteries'. There is, as you would expect in Adnams' country, a lovely village church and a sixteenth-century Wattisfield Hall, a fragment of the story that the village decided to publish entitled *A Short History of Wattisfield*.

Compiled by the Wattisfield Millennium Village Book Committee, it deals with life and work in the village from the earliest times.

Because of its rich source of mica clay, Wattisfield has been known for its pottery since Bronze Age times; the Roman settlement there had twenty or more kilns and the early track along which supplies of clay were brought from the Caulke Wood into the settlement has been clearly traced.

Set in rich agricultural country, farming was a major occupation too; there is no doubt that up to 1800 Wattisfield would have been self-sufficient and served by a wide variety of traders and craftsmen. Many would show more than one occupation such as 'pottery manufacturer and farmer'.

Thomas Watson began in business in 1800 when he bought a pottery with land and a dairy. Shrewd and innovative, he and successive generations of the family exploited every opportunity to expand: the opening of Finningham rail station in 1849 and the availability of coal for kilns made firing much more economical.

There was at least one other potter at Wattisfield, but it was Watson's business that flourished – at least until the First World War, when wartime needs such as land drain pipes became a priority; labour was difficult to find, though. After the war, Watson's turned to the production of flower pots, reaching a high level of production using new kilns and drying sheds.

The Brick Kiln in the Pottery Yard was built by staff in the evenings in 1940/1941 and was used up to 1963 when a fire totally destroyed the pottery premises. Throughout its use, the kiln fired a weekly load of about 5,000 pieces, mainly flower pots; it has been suitably restored, near to the rebuilt factory premises.

After the fire the new kilns were fired by electricity, able to take advantage of new conditions and to move into the production of domestic ware and specialist designs required by a developing world market. Such was the size of the global market that Henry Watson Potteries needed to collaborate with potteries in Stoke on Trent and Portugal to cope with the demand.

The kiln for Henry Watson's Potteries at Wattisfield has been restored.

A Roman kiln offers an interesting comparison.

Watson's have been at Wattisfield for over 200 years now: some achievement! Look for the brown sign pointing to the Potteries which are on the east side of the A143 about halfway between Bury St Edmunds and the Scole roundabout. A steep curving entrance drive leads up to the Potteries with a car park to the rear.

The Potteries shop has a wide range of domestic ware, particularly for the kitchen and the dining table; look no further for the smart kitchen gear worn by so many 'family' chefs. While browsing for books, cards and calendars look for *The Brick Kiln,* a (free) illustrated handout produced by Henry Watson's, giving a fascinating account of its operation.

At the rear of the pottery shop is one other 'place to be': go there! The coffee and sponge cake are truly to die for.

Directions:

A14 to Bury St Edmunds Junction 43 then A143 east. Wattisfield about 8 miles
or
A14 north of Ipswich to Junction 47 then right A1088
At Ickworth roundabout right to Wattisfield on A143

Adnams' pub:

Gladstone Arms   Combs Ford, Stowmarket   01449 612339

5

The Wool Towns

Clare, Cavendish, Long Melford, Sudbury, Lavenham, Kersey and Hadleigh; names to conjure with, memories to treasure. Like pearls on a necklace, these examples of medieval England at its finest appear one after another along the banks of the River Stour and its tributaries.

The Stour is a border river, rising on the margin of Suffolk and Cambridgeshire, forming the Suffolk-Essex border along most of its length and joining the Orwell in the wide North Sea estuary. Different from any other part of Adnams Country the Stour Valley has become a paradise for the photographer and historian, and a source of wonder for visitors able to see this gentle countryside and its villages as it was 500 years ago. Sheep grazed on the lush water meadows, cloth making brought prosperity and huge churches and guildhalls were built.

Mercifully, when the Industrial Revolution came, factory production established itself in the north near the source of power: coal. The wool towns of Suffolk were left preserved and untouched by industrial developments; there was hardship, of course, but the buildings of medieval England with their half-timbered houses – whole streets of them – survived.

A Word About Pargetting

Pargetting is a form of artwork that became very popular in the sixteenth century; timber framed buildings covered with plaster needed some form of decoration. Even when timber studs had been left visible the plaster panels between them were often patterned.

Some of the patterns were scratched on to the plaster surface, others were impressed; moulded versions created in high relief sometimes illustrated legendary figures. Fine examples of this are found on the Ancient House at Ipswich and on the former Sun Inn at Saffron Walden in Essex. Because the weight of the plaster could result in its falling away from the backing there are few of these highly decorated surfaces left.

The plaster used for pargetting consisted of lime and sand, bound together with animal fat, hair, straw and cow dung. The mixture was spread on to horizontal laths fixed close together across the timber frame of a building. While still soft, the surface was given its decoration, common designs being wavy lines, chevrons, geometric patterns, shells and scrolls.

Although pargetting was seen as an alternative to the colouring of plaster walls, many people gave their decoration a colourwash too, often the traditional 'Suffolk pink'.

Fortunately there are craftsmen – just a few – who are able to repair existing pargetted walls and to use old methods to create patterns on modern plaster walls. The modern plaster recipe is made stronger than the sixteenth-century one by the addition of a trace of cement, although it tends to crack more easily.

Cavendish

Village greens are a traditional feature of the English countryside; that at Cavendish is unforgettable. Backed by a little group of colour washed, thatched cottages (Hyde Park Corner) and the tower of St Mary's Church, this part of Adnams Country is real England. There are five almshouses in this group; for many years a 'not so new' man's cycle was always to be seen leaning against the wall of the corner cottage. When one day it had gone, people began to ask if tragedy had struck until there was comforting news, 'The bike's back'...

Many visitors to the village already know that the Duke of Devonshire's family name is derived from Cavendish. Ownership of the manor passed by marriage to Sir John Cavendish in the fourteenth century and remained in the family until it was sold by William Cavendish in 1569.

The manor house, Overhall, the Cavendish family home, stood at the end of a long drive close to the church and the green. For some years it was owned by the church and when a new rectory was built, 'old' Overhall was demolished in 1895; only a fragment remains. The old rectory across the green and close to the pond became the headquarters of the Sue Ryder Foundation; now empty, it is protected, but the site is scheduled for development. The Sue Ryder shop occupies the Old Cinema opposite Hyde Park Corner.

A little further beyond Overhall, at the corner of Colts Hill Road is Nether Hall, a sixteenth-century timber framed, oversailed farmhouse with a fine two-storey porch. For some years there was a winery there, popular with visitors, but that has closed down.

The church was built in the 1300s, flint being extensively used, the tower having a prominent stair turret. The stained glass was smashed during the Commonwealth, but there is much flushwork, particularly round the clerestory windows of the nave. The chancel was built through the will of Sir John Cavendish, who was murdered by rebels during the Peasants' Revolt in 1381.

The font is octagonal with a panelled stem; the bowl is decorated with signs of the Evangelists. Of the monuments, that for Sir George Colt is outstanding and is dated 1570.

Just beyond Adnams' Bull Inn (lunch was memorable) is the village post office where a book published by the Cavendish Book Project is available, also a hand drawn map of the village (£1) which identifies all the buildings. Look for the Maltings and Cavendish House on the left; further along and opposite the Memorial Hall is Pentlow Lane with the Old Railway Arms on the corner.

Just a few yards down the lane on the left is a garden with the old station platform revealing fairly recent history; the crossing gates stood nearby, the Stour Valley line track going along the bank of the river as it does at Clare.

Cavendish Green with Hyde Park Corner cottages – an incomparable view.

The Stour Valley line passed through the castle grounds at Clare.

The old railway bridge of the Stour Valley line still stands at Rodbridge.

1. Bury Abbey's north transept's size shows the grandeur of the building, begun in 1080.

2. Of all Suffolk's massive churches, that of St Edmund, Southwold, is is one of the most magnificent with extensive use of flushwork. Its dedication is significant.

3. Such is the demand for a beach hut at Southwold that there is a frantic rush when one becomes available.

4. Christchurch Mansion and Park at Ipswich are open to the public as an art gallery and open space, given to the town by Felix Thornley Cobbold, a local businessman.

5. Aerial view of the Bawdsey Estate. (Courtesy of the Bawdsey Manor Estate)

6. The south front of Bawdsey Manor. (Courtesy of the Bawdsey Manor Estate)

7. Looking south from Bawdsey Manor. (Courtesy of the Bawdsey Manor Estate)

8. Helmingham Hall Gardens. The house is not open to the public, but the gardens are open at weekends and are a delight, setting a standard for other houses to follow.

9. Melford Hall. (The National Trust)

10. Otley Hall, a perfect example of a small moated house. It is open to the public and serves as a religious 'retreat'. Images here include the hall seen from the moat, the Great Hall and the Linenfold Room.

11. The Great Hall, Otley Hall.

12. The Linenfold Room, Otley Hall..

13. The Gloster Javelin is one of the museum's advanced aircraft and is kept in a 'ready for action' condition. (Norfolk & Suffolk Aviation Museum)

14. A painting of Charles II at Euston Hall. (Courtesy of the Duke of Grafton)

15. Aldeburgh beach is not only picturesque; buy your fish from the boats and get them fresh!

16. Orford Castle, a revolutionary keep design, stands on a mound overlooking the sea.

17. Blythburgh Parish Church is magnificent, especially when seen floodlit from the south.

18. The Great Hall at Melford Hall originally had a traditional screen across it. The stairs that replaced it have transformed its appearance. (Courtesy of The National Trust)

19. The peaceful coastline at Dunwich has a tragic history to tell.

20. Herringfleet Smock Mill has been restored and is in action from time to time.

21. The Wenhaston 'Doom' is an outstanding example of belief in the judgement as understood by early Christians.

22. Parham's defensive moat could only be crossed through a massive gateway.

23. Remote and beautiful, South Elmham was once a bishop's seat around 680.

24. Here, the Mill Stream at Flatford joins the main river below Willy Lott's house.

25. John Constable's parents are buried in East Bergholt Churchyard.

26. The Red Lion at Great Wrtting has a massive whalebone arch framing its door..

27. Flatford Mill was owned by John Constable's father, Golding.

28. The classic view of the river at Flatford.

29. Dedham had a flourishing community of weavers; this is Southfields.

It is worth going a few yards further and walking along the raised footpath (clearly the river floods here) to look at the attractive group of eighteenth-century buildings at Pentlow Mill. The Essex county sign is on the bend of the road close to the entrance to the mill.

Adnams' pub:

The Bull   The Street, Cavendish   01787 280245

Clare

Clare is a fine example of visual history and for visitors to the wool towns, the first to explore when travelling downstream from the river's source north of Haverhill. It may also be an introduction to a form of external house decoration only found in eastern England and in particular in this part of Adnams Country. Such is the history and beauty of this decorative plasterwork, pargetting, that a special account appears at the beginning of this chapter.

The Earls of Clare became a powerful family, having been granted the land here by William the Conqueror after the battle of Hastings; their name came from the village which was the centre of the Honour of Clare, the extensive land holdings and manor houses of the family and their supporters.

The Clares founded an Augustinian Priory close to the river at Clare; like other religious houses it became ruined after the Dissolution of the Monasteries, but the Friars returned in 1953 and occupy the still-standing Prior's Lodging.

The male line of Clares died out at Bannockburn in 1314, but there was a surviving sister who founded Clare College, Cambridge (earlier known as University Hall).

Weaving became a flourishing cottage industry in Clare, but of equal importance was local agriculture and markets for cereals and livestock. The wealth that resulted went into the building of the lovely church of St Peter and St Paul and its later restoration. It is easily recognisable from its profile that shows prominent twin rood turrets with decorated caps at the junction of nave and choir. The medieval stained glass was smashed by William Dowsing, but the fan vaulting of the south porch remains, also fragments of the rood screen.

On the south side of the church is the Ancient House, often called the Priest's House with extraordinary pargetting on the side and gable end, carrying the date 1473. There are many houses of interest along the High Street and Nethergate Street, its extension to the south west. Look for Nethergate House on the left; on the right are Georgian houses of quality and Netheridge, a gable-ended building simply covered with moulded pargetting in plant forms. At one time this was colour washed in avocado – perhaps to match the bathroom! In due course reason prevailed and it was recoloured in 'Suffolk pink'.

At the crossroads there is a sign to the castle, also built by the Clares. The views from the top are excellent, but only a small part of the defensive keep is left. Below in the bailey, or courtyard, was Clare Railway Station, once a stop on the Stour Valley railway line which ran through the site; this provided a route from Long Melford though Clare to Haverhill and Cambridge, but was closed in 1967.

The platforms and station building are still there, also the goods shed, all part of a visitors' centre and a Country Park – a peaceful and beautiful picnic spot by the river. The former railway bridge carries a public footpath leading to the Priory.

North of the parish church, High Street and Market Street join and continue into Callis Street, a reference to a fourteenth-century law requiring wool exporters to use the port of Calais, then under the English crown. Warehouses for this were known as Callises, so it's likely that there was one nearby.

One of several attractive pubs in Clare is Adnams' Cock Inn in Callis Street; almost opposite is Grove House, easily recognisable with its five gables and nineteenth-century pillared door.

Clare's Ancient House is a marvel of pargetting, dated 1473.

The house dates from the fourteenth century and as a farmhouse on some 130 acres with its own maltings it must have been owned by a wealthy family.

Adnams' pubs:

Cock Inn	Clare	01787 277391
Red Lion	Great Wratting	01440 783237
The Bull	Cavendish	01787 280245

Hadleigh

Although Hadleigh was not the largest of the wool towns, it was one of the more important and one in five of the male population was employed in the woollen industry. The River Brett has, upstream, the delightful village of Kersey with its watersplash; downstream the Brett joins the Stour at Higham, where Constable Country begins.

The river provided Hadleigh with water for washing wool and fulling cloth, for transport and, later, with power for its mills; in early days industry was cottage-based. Prosperity came from wool to Hadleigh, as the high quality of many of the houses in and around the High Street shows; good examples of pargetting can be seen here, as they are in other places such as Clare. Look for overhanging eaves and carved brackets, too.

Of the historic buildings in the town, one of the most attractive is Toppesfield Bridge, just off the High Street, where Duke Street crosses the River Brett. It was built in the fourteenth century and is the oldest bridge in the county still in use; with the development of road traffic it had to be enlarged to twice its original width.

Nearby, are Hadleigh's major architecturally important buildings, each with a story to tell.

St Mary's Church is the fifth church of the county in size, the oldest part being the thirteenth-century flint tower with a 135ft timber-framed, lead-covered spire. The chancel roof has rich tracery and in the north wall is an Easter sepulchre; during the fifteenth century when

Hadleigh was at its most prosperous, the church was enlarged and a special entrance built for the use of the important medieval guilds in the town.

In the sanctuary of the chapel at the east end of the south aisle is a bench carved with an animal holding a man's head in its teeth. It represents the head of King (later Saint) Edmund, who was killed and decapitated by the Danes in 870. The king's followers were unable to find his body until they were attracted by the cries of a wolf they found guarding it.

In a window of the south wall is a group of scenes in the life of Rowland Taylor who was appointed to the living of Hadleigh by Archbishop Cranmer. The Reformation was actively developing in the town and Taylor became well-loved; during the reign of Mary Tudor when Protestants were being persecuted he found a priest celebrating the Roman Catholic Mass in his church and ejected him, only to be arrested himself and condemned to death. He was burned at the stake on Aldham Common where a monument to him stands across a field a mile or so along the Ipswich Road.

The fifteenth-century timber-framed Guildhall is on the south side of the church and was the meeting place of the five guilds which existed at Hadleigh; it was built as a market hall with medieval shops on the ground floor. Behind is the original Guildhall, the upper chamber being known as the Old Town Hall.

Anyone interested in the work of medieval craftsmen should go to see the open crown- post roofs and the great beams, especially in the Guild Room. Over the centuries the building has housed schools, almshouses and a workhouse; today the Guildhall Town Hall Complex is held in trust for the town, the rooms being rented out for community use.

The Deanery Tower faces the west end of the church. Built of red brick in 1495 it was the great gateway to the palace of Archdeacon Pykenham that stood near the river.

It has ornate chimneys and octagonal battlemented turrets on either side of the doorway that reach well above roof level. The palace was demolished, but the tower remains; in one of the rooms in the Tower, Dean Rose held a conference in 1833 which was to lead to the Oxford Movement. One of the main objects of this was to promote the return of ritual and colour to services in the Church of England.

Hadleigh's Church and Deanery Tower are harmonious neighbours.

The church has one of Suffolk's many representations of the story of St Edmund and the wolf.

In and around the Market Place are other, more modern buildings of note: the Corn Exchange, the new Town Hall and on High Street close to the end of Church Street, the medieval George Inn.

Rich as Hadleigh is in its historic buildings in the old part of town, care has been taken to preserve much of the town's nineteenth-century railway. Only 7½ miles of track linking Hadleigh and Bentley Junction were laid, mainly to serve the local industries such as milling and malting. (see Lost Railways p. 143)

Fortunately, instead of being neglected or forgotten – or even ploughed over – the railway track at Hadleigh was recognised as an asset and is now a Local Nature Reserve owned and managed by Babergh District Council.

The 2½ mile railway walk between Hadleigh and Raydon Old Station passes through a variety of landscapes; because of the abundance of food and nest sites birds find this protected track an ideal habitat. In the summer months blossom attracts butterflies of all kinds and there are even cultivated apple trees where orchards once bordered the track.

The Hadleigh Walk is part of the National Cycle Network supported by SUSTRANS, a charity that works to encourage people to walk, cycle and use public transport in order to reduce motor traffic. The Hadleigh Walk is open to both horse riders and cyclists and there are small car parks at both Hadleigh and Raydon stations.

An unusual landmark stands where footpaths meet soon after leaving Hadleigh: the waypost sculpture, one of 1,000 designs funded by the Royal Bank of Scotland. The distances shown on its arm are: Hadleigh ½ mile and Raydon 1½ miles. Just beyond the last house is the curiously named 'The Fuzz', a depression of over 4 acres, probably once a sand pit, valuable in the past for many purposes, such as building work. Much excavation work was done at the Hadleigh end of the track particularly to form sidings – so – called 'cut and fill' and it is still possible to follow the line of cuttings and embankments that were constructed.

The housing development round the former Hadleigh Station merits an award: the Mill and Granary are now handsome apartments and the whole area is now complete with attractive modern houses. One road which is part of the development has been named 'The Granary'; next to it is 'Station Yard' at the end of which is the former Hadleigh station building still thankfully in good condition with its original canopy. Judging by the garden games equipment it was being used in 2007 as a Day Nursery.

Hadleigh Railway Walk is a project of which the town should be proud and no visitor should miss. It is a great day out.

Directions:

Railway Walk:

Take High Street B1070 South
At the end of Station Road follow brown signs to Railway Walk
Station Yard leads to former station building

Hadleigh:

A12 to Ipswich, then A1071 to Hadleigh
or
A14 to Bury St Edmunds, then A134/A1141 to Hadleigh

Adnams' pubs:

The Bull	The Street, Cavendish	01787 280245
The Cock Inn	3 Callis Street, Clare	01787277391

Kersey

There used to be a Kersey Cloth back in the days when the village was part of the Stour Valley textile area. Then the villagers worked with local wool to produce broadcloth in their homes; textiles have gone now, but Kersey remains, held by many to be the most beautiful village in Suffolk, in England even?

Its original name 'Carseye' came from 'Island on the Car', the stream on which Kersey stood and which still joins the River Brett; it was essential for washing wool. The watersplash crossed by the road or the road crossed by the stream is a reminder of the old cloth-making days and always attracts photographers. There is always a temptation to wait for still water and reflections, particularly of the church on the hill above. But be warned: ducks have priority, cars do have to pass through and the village boys in their wellies love the water. Have patience!

Park the car and walk: enjoy the colour washed cottages and their colourful gardens, admire the timber framing, the Old Bell Inn, the Tudor River House with a brick porch and cross the watersplash by the footbridge.

The view from the church over the village is exceptional, but its age is exceptional too. The nave was built in 1335, the tower in 1481, the church far bigger than Kersey's needs.

The south porch is a beautiful example of flushwork and has a carved roof divided into sixteen panels covered with elaborate tracery. Although the interior of the church suffered from damage at the Reformation and later restoration, a real treasure survived: six panels of the fifteenth-century rood screen and still in the original colours. The screen shows the figures of three prophets and three kings; one of these is St Edmund with the arrow that is a memorial to his martyrdom in 870, symbolised in so many places in Suffolk such as St Edmundsbury, Southwold, Hadleigh and Hoxne.

Kersey's watersplash and its
reflections are known worldwide.

Lavenham

If any wool town had to stand as a symbol of them all it would be Lavenham – a real survivor
of medieval times – its original streets lined with timber-framed houses and the magnificent
Guildhall of Corpus Christi dominating the Market Place. The wealth that cloth making
brought to Lavenham can be seen all around, not least in the building of the church of St Peter
and St Paul.

Lavenham's reputation was built upon its broadcloth. In the fourteenth century during the
100 Years War, many Flemish weavers emigrated and settled in the Stour Valley, particularly
at Lavenham, bringing their skills of fine weaving with them. Street and family names are a
reminder of that: Prentice Street and Shilling (Schylling) Grange.

The wealthiest of the 'wool men' were the clothiers who traded and financed all stages of the
cloth production from spinning to the finished product. By 1520 Lavenhams's prosperity was
legendary, but then the broadcloth industry began to collapse: war interrupted trade and on the
Continent, new, lighter cloths began to be produced and became very popular.

For a while Lavenham's textile industry survived by turning to the so-called 'New Draperies',
but the development of water power, the invention of textile machinery for factory production
meant the end. Steam power took the industry to the north where there was coal, leaving
Lavenham untouched by the dirt and squalor of the Industrial Revolution.

Controlling the medieval textile industry and carrying out important religious functions
were the Guildhalls of which the survivor is the Guildhall of Corpus Christi. It was built in
1528 and was the centre regulating textiles in the town until the Dissolution; after the industry

collapsed it was used as a town hall, a prison, and a workhouse. Today it is in the care of The National Trust and is open to the public. Its long front is jettied; there is a two-storeyed porch and elaborate carvings; that on the corner post represents John de Vere, 15th Earl of Oxford, founder of the Guild.

Downstairs is a large hall; smaller rooms are occupied by the library and upstairs is an excellent museum.

A small building nearby is Little Hall, a fifteenth-century hall house, gabled, with diagonal timber braces; this is the headquarters of the Suffolk Preservation Society. From the corner of the Guildhall is Lady Street with a former shop at the corner with Water Street. Built in Tudor times, customers outside were served from inside through arched window spaces. On the opposite corner is the Wool Hall, originally the hall of the Guild of the Blessed Virgin (hence Lady Street). It was later divided into three houses and is now incorporated into the Swan Hotel as the residents' lounge; it has a fine crown-post roof.

Water Street together with Barn Street and Shilling Street leading off it have many medieval buildings of interest. The Priory and the de Vere House are the most prominent, although the latter was substantially rebuilt in the twentieth century. All the streets have weaver's cottages as well as larger houses of the wealthier textile people: the Suffolk Preservation Society's *A Walk around Lavenham* is invaluable when visiting the town. Leaning gables and ancient shop fronts line the High Street from the Swan, with narrow Market Lane leading back into the Market Place.

From the Swan at the corner of Water Street the next essential walk is along Church Street (there is a convenient car park half way to the church). Many visitors to Lavenham will have driven from Long Melford and have seen the church tower appear suddenly as if by magic, isolated against the skyline – this is a real experience. The church is on the edge of town, but there are attractive homes opposite and further along Church Street towards the car park. The path to the church is from the south east, giving an incomparable view of its whole length and the tower.

Expense was no object when the Church of St Peter and St Paul was built in 1485. It is not just the 141ft tower that shows this, but the lavish use of stone from the Stamford area, brought by sea and river at great cost. Flint was extensively used of course, particularly on the tower,

Lavenham is full of historic timbered buildings, none more attractive than the Guildhall.

Long Melford Church is one of the
great 'wool' churches of Suffolk.

William Cordell's tomb in Long
Melford Church has a special beauty.

but the nave is faced with stone, the south porch is entirely of stone and windows, arches and buttresses are framed with it: perfect examples of flushwork.

The cost of the new church was borne by two men: the Lord of the Manor, John de Vere, 13th Earl of Oxford newly returned from the Battle of Bosworth, where he fought for Henry VII, and Thomas Spring II, a rich local merchant. Their marks are prominent on the church: look for the mullet, or 5-pointed star, badge of the de Veres high up on the tower and round its base, where it alternates with the Spring coat of arms, which also appears round the top of the tower.

Building work was continued by successive generations of the families during the peak of Lavenham's prosperity, but when textiles in the town declined it stopped and the chancel was left unaltered.

The south, or de Vere porch has their star all over it and fan vaulting in its roof; work of the masons is enhanced in the nave following the destruction of its stained glass by Dowsing, which allows light to flood in.

The woodwork is of superb quality: tie beams in the roof are decorated with angels and the rood screen of 1330 has delicately carved flowers, foliage and human heads. Below the choir stalls are misericords; look for Pelican in her Piety and the Musicians, which are of special interest. Most impressive of all are parcloses (wooden enclosures) made to contain tombs; the carving is lace-like in its detail, especially on the screens for the Spring and Oxford chantries where Masses and prayers were said for the departed.

Adnams' pubs:

Cock Inn	Clare	01787 277391
Red Lion	Great Wratting	01440 783237

Long Melford

Even among the wool towns, Long Melford is exceptional in the richness of its buildings and the beauty of their setting. The huge Green seems to have attracted to itself as much as the mind and eye can grasp; the first sight of the church of the Holy Trinity is alone enough to capture the imagination.

There are those who suggest exploring the treasures around the Green straight away on arrival at Long Melford to make the whole seem believable; the contrary view is to walk from the south end of the mile-long High Street to make the buildings round the Green the climax - rather like reaching the Great Hall at the end of a visit to a great historic house.

The High Street has much interest in itself: there are the antique and craft establishments, of course, but also many traditional inns and shops to meet local day to day needs. Medieval and Tudor timbered buildings are in the majority, but Georgian styles are there too, as well as Victorian 'in fills'. Red brick and Suffolk white (grey really) add even more variety to the scene, yet retaining a harmonious whole.

Towards the north end of the High Street is the famous sixteenth-century timbered Bull Inn followed by the bridge where, in the old days there was a ford. Beyond is the vast triangular Green, bordered on the left by houses and cottages with lovely gardens; on the right is the high wall of Melford Hall. Above it is a glimpse of the hall's octagonal turrets and the pointed gables of the garden house, or gazebo. Now in the care of The National Trust, the house is the home of the Hyde Parker family.

The old manor house that stood here was the property of the Abbots of St Edmundsbury, but following the Dissolution of the Monasteries was granted by the King to William Cordell, a brilliant lawyer at Court who later became Speaker of the House of Commons and Master of the Rolls. As Sir William he rebuilt the Hall between 1554 and 1578 and entertained Queen Elizabeth I there on one of her progresses.

Melford Hall. (NT/Fisheye Images)

Melford Hall. The brick for the building was taken from clay on the green opposite. (NT/Fisheye Images)

The property passed down the female line and was finally sold to the Parker family in 1786, then became the home of the Hyde Parkers. Although there was a serious fire in 1942, repairs and restoration have returned the house to its normal immaculate condition.

The exterior is in warm red brick, the clay being taken from the Green nearby. Two wings of the house stretch eastward forming an open court; an old plan shows an eastern wing that enclosed the courtyard completely.

A number of interior alterations have been made over the centuries, including the replacement of the traditional screens passage at the service end of the Banqueting Hall by columns framing stairs that lead to a columned gallery. The architect for this work in 1813 was Thomas Hopper. The Banqueting Hall has family portraits and valuable antique furniture. Also by Thomas Hopper was a Regency Library. Naval memorabilia are a reminder of the Hyde Parker naval connections.

The garden and the Garden Room should not be missed: the eight pointed gables and corner shafts are crowned with tall finials.

On the Green the only building is the water conduit above the spring that supplied the Hall, but looking down on the Green is a crowning glory: the church of the Holy Trinity, its surrounding cottages and houses and the Trinity Hospital, almshouses founded by Sir William Cordell in 1573. In red brick, much restoration was done to them in the nineteenth century.

Holy Trinity Church: to the left of the almshouses Church Walk opens up to a wonderful view of the south side of the church. It was a 'new' church in 1460, but its tower is not old at all. The original was struck by lightning in 1710 and a replacement for it was built soon afterwards. This seems to have been inadequate in every way; fortunately the present tower was built round it in 1903, as handsome as any of the great church towers of the wool towns.

The view of Long Melford Church from the south east shows the nave windows to perfection: an enormous range of eighteen clerestory windows, allowing the light to stream in above the main twelve nave windows. Flint and freestone provide the surface texture and decoration for the south wall, the parapets being battlemented. At the east end, a lower, three-gabled building is the Lady Chapel.

Looking down inside the nave with its high roof, slender pillars and high pointed arches to the east window, the open space is emphasised by the lack of a chancel arch: an example of a 'hall' church, a feature of East Anglia.

Fortunately the original stained glass is still in the north aisle; in so many churches it was destroyed by the Puritans. Close to the Clopton Chantry Chapel is a treasure in the north wall dating from about 1350; an alabaster relief of the Adoration of the Magi. The tomb of Sir William Clopton, father of John Clopton of Kentwell, who founded the church is nearby. John's tomb is just to the left of the high altar.

To the right of the altar is the tomb of Sir William Cordell who died at Melford Hall in 1581. If it looks familiar, you may have been to Stamford where there is a similar (but larger) tomb for William Cecil, Lord Burghley, Elizabeth I's 'first minister'.

Entrance to the Lady Chapel (1496) is outside the church; in the centre it has a cloister, or ambulatory. The chapel was used as a village school from 1670 and the evidence for this is the multiplication table on the wall.

Sudbury

Wartime pupils of Leiston Grammar School remember Sudbury with particular affection, as they had such a warm welcome from Sudbury people when their school was evacuated 'en bloc' to the town in the summer of 1940 to escape the daily dangers on the east coast. Distances do not seem so great now, but Sudbury in those days was a world very few, if any, had seen before their arrival.

They did their exploring on bicycles both in town and in the countryside. If you ask them what they remember most about Sudbury they will say Market Hill and St Peter's Church.

St Peter's Church
on the Market
Place at Sudbury
has a striking
statue of Thomas
Gainsborough.

Market Hill has been a Market Place since the fourteenth century and markets are still held there on Thursdays and Saturdays. St Peter's is now redundant, but is used extensively for concerts and exhibitions.

A statue of Thomas Gainsborough stands at the west end of the church; beyond Market Hill, Gainsborough Street continues towards the painter's birthplace, Gainsborough House, where there is an excellent gallery and an attractive garden. Leiston pupils already aware of John Constable and Constable Country close by were soon introduced to the work of Suffolk's other great painter, whose father John was a clothier in Sudbury.

Thomas was John Gainsborough's youngest son who was born in the house in 1727; his exceptional talent led him, like John Constable, to landscape painting. But painting actual scenes as Constable did was not for him; he was more interested in mood and effect such as glowing dawns and sunsets.

With the help of a legacy from a relative, Thomas went to London and joined a French engraver, Gravelot; while there he married beautiful Margaret Burr, the illegitimate daughter of the Duke of Beaufort. Her annuity helped to support their growing family and Gainsborough

Like Lavenham, Sudbury was a busy weaving centre. Salter's Hall is one of the many attractive timbered houses (1450).

became involved in portraiture which brought him wealth. The family moved to Ipswich, then to Bath, where his portraits became very popular.

Such was Gainsborough's fame that he became a founder member of the Royal Academy. Gainsborough House has the largest collection of his work anywhere and no visitor to Sudbury should miss the opportunity to see it.

Gainsborough Street continues into Stour Street, where there are some splendid timbered merchants' houses. Sudbury was the largest of the Wool Towns; the size and quality of The Chantry and of Salter's Hall in Stour Street show how important the town became. Workers were attracted there and delightful weavers' cottages remain, too.

Without water to wash wool and to dye cloth, a textile industry would not be possible and any visit to Sudbury should include the Croft and St Gregory's Church, other features remembered by the 1940 evacuees. Parking at the Croft is one of the great pleasures of a visit to Sudbury; under the trees fringing the wide green sloping down to the river it seems perfection. Across a little footbridge is Mill Acre and a picnic place.

Only a few steps across the green is St Gregory's Church, where there is a huge fifteenth-century font cover; its carving is not the only example in the church as there are fine misericords as well. Pride of place at St Gregory's must go to its carved and painted roofs. In the chancel is one beauty, while the whole of the bay at the eastern end of the nave has a roof decorated to serve as a canopy of honour for the rood and for a nave altar.

Walking by the river is a particularly enjoyable way of seeing Sudbury. I enjoy the Quay Theatre, a restored Georgian warehouse, where there are regular dramatic and musical events. The bar upstairs is open at lunch times and in the evenings and art exhibitions take place there.

Just out of town on the way to Long Melford is the Rodbridge Picnic Site, where there are riverside walks; still standing and in good condition is the railway bridge that once carried the Stour Valley line over the river.

Although few guide books give it a mention, the tiny village of Bures only five miles south of Sudbury on the B1508 has the chapel of St Stephen, the place where Edmund was crowned king in 855. (see p 17) The walk to the chapel is magic.

Sudbury's Quay Theatre, a much–loved restoration.

The story of his martyrdom at the hands of the Danes and the beliefs that grew around this tragic event have to be told separately, as they involve the village of Hoxne (pronounced Hoxen) far away on the Suffolk/Norfolk border. (see p. 138) As usual, road directions are included, as railways are thin on the ground in Suffolk.

The railway links from Sudbury to Bury St Edmunds and to Cambridge have gone, but there is still a service to Marks Tey and connections there on the main line to London, Liverpool Street.

Directions:

A12 to Colchester then A134
or
A14 to Bury St Edmunds; at Junction 44 take the A134
For parking follow signs for Town Hall
Information Tourist Information Centre at Town Hall

Adnams' pubs:

The Bull	The Street, Cavendish	01787 280245
The Cock Inn	3 Callis Street, Clare	01787 277391

6

Rivers Blyth and Yox

Blythburgh

There are two views here that need to seen to be believed. One is the extraordinary display of rhododendrons in Henham woods along the A12 north of the village and especially beside the A145 Beccles Road. Visit at rhododendron time, of course. The second is the floodlit view of Holy Trinity Church at night approaching Bythburgh from the south.

The church has suffered violence since its building in the early 1400s, damage in a fire in 1438 was followed a great storm in 1577 that caused the spire to fall through the roof. In those days superstition was strong; many believed that the Devil had visited the church and killed two of the congregation. Worshippers said that a huge black dog sprang from the roof and left scorch marks by the door. The dog is said to have been at St Mary's in Bungay and in other places in Suffolk.

It is a vast church, built to be seen from the south where it is at its best with its battlemented nave parapet, fine porch and its great row of eighteen clerestory windows. Viewed from the marshes to the north its comparative plain appearance makes it seem almost a different church.

The interior is spacious and like many East Anglian churches there is no arch between nave and chancel; a so-called hall church. Terrible damage was done by Dowsing and his followers in 1644; statues were destroyed, horses were stabled in the nave and glass was smashed. Shots were fired everywhere, especially to damage the painted rafters and the beautifully coloured angels fixed to each of the beams of the roof. Thankfully the carved bench ends survived; their 'poppy heads' wonderfully representing the seven deadly sins, also the fifteenth-century lectern and the rare Jack o' the Clock. (There is also one at St Edmunds, Southwold).

Blythburgh benefited when Dunwich lost its harbour (see p. 116); ships came instead to Blythburgh and berthed in increasing numbers along the quay there. Trade was good, but a fire in 1676 swept through the village, destroying the market place, public buildings and an inn. The present White Hart with its Dutch-styled gable end was one of the survivors and continued to serve as a court house. Today it is a favourite Adnams' pub; not only is it in a convenient location on the road to the coast, but it has retained its traditional interior. There are original carved oak beams, a massive open fireplace with inglenook chimney, an attractive restaurant as well as a bar and accommodation for residents.

Visitors to Blythburgh have a choice of countryside walks that are the envy of other villages. To the west is common land leading to Wenhaston; alternatively one can follow a path north of the church up river that provides a contrasting landscape. Easterly towards Walberswick there are nature reserves and bird sanctuaries on the south of the estuary.

This is Sandling country, once forested and later grazed by sheep and cattle. The light soil lost its nutrients through grazing and low rainfall until little will grow now apart from gorse and bracken; the area became of little value for agriculture, but has been a good source of sand and gravel.

The sign at the B1387 turning about a mile south of Blythburgh points to a picnic site called Toby's Walks; there, paths thread their way through clumps of brilliant yellow gorse. The marked walks from the car park explore the hills and hollows that represent the old excavations for sand and gravel. Unusual and now so colourful it is difficult to imagine that a gibbet once stood here.

Blythburgh's carving on the choir stalls is superb.

The Angel Roof at Blythburgh is one of the wonders of this village church.

Legend has it that Tobias Gill, a soldier camped at Blythburgh in 1750, attacked and murdered a local girl, Ann Blakemore while he was wandering drunk across the Common. He was convicted of the murder and hanged at Toby's Walks, hence the name. There are those who say he still wanders here, but like the gibbet he seems to have vanished.

Adnams' pubs:

White Hart	London Road, Blythburgh	01502 478217 (Accomm)
Queen's Head	Halesworth Road, Blyford	01502 478404 (Accomm)

Holton, Blyford and Wenhaston

East from Halesworth, the B1123 enters Holton quickly. On the high ground overlooking the village is one of Suffolk's famous post mills dating from 1752. Now restored, it has a round house, white painted body and four sails. Visits can be arranged by calling 01986 872367.

Next along the B1123 comes Blyford (historically Blythford), at the curve of the road where the sign points to Wenhaston is Adnams' Queen's Head and what a picture it makes! The queen's head on the pub sign is that of the wife of the Christian King Anna; he is supposed to have been killed at a seventh-century battle at nearby Bulcamp. There is no evidence for this, but local belief is strong.

Wenhaston is quickly reached from the turning at Blyford and the journey is certainly worthwhile to see the remarkable 'Doom' in St Peter's Church. This is a rood-screen painting of the Last Judgement thought to have been completed in about 1520; a Dutch hand is believed to have been responsible, although another theory is that a local monk painted it.

It is on wooden panels and shows Christ in Glory, flanked by the Blessed Virgin Mary and St John. St Michael is shown weighing souls and St Peter holds the key to Heaven, while the terrors of Hell are vividly portrayed.

Its survival as one of the finest Doom paintings in the country was made possible when it was covered by whitewash by order of Parliament in 1545. It would otherwise have been destroyed by zealous commissioners during the Commonwealth.

Miracles can happen; in the course of restoration in the nineteenth century the panels were taken down and put in the churchyard, perhaps destined as firewood. Heavy overnight rain washed off the whitewash and the Doom could be seen again. It is now on the north wall of the church, facing the door: don't miss it.

Adnams' pubs:

Queen's Head	Halesworth Road, Blyford	01502 478404 (Accomm)
Star Inn	Hall Road, Wenhaston	01502 478240
Angel Hotel	The Thoroughfare, Halesworth	01986 873365 (Accomm)
White Hart	The Thoroughfare, Halesworth	01986 873386

Walberswick

It is a peculiarity of this part of the east coast that to reach a number of the seaside villages there is only one access and exit road. Leaving the A12 just south of Blythburgh a landmark at the next crossroads is a water tower; beyond it the only destination can be Walberswick. The Blyth estuary is close by to the north, Westwood Marshes are to the south and at Walberswick is the sea shore.

This is good walking country: heath land with gorse and bracken, the old railway track to follow, or along Tinker's Walks through the heather. The landscape is virtually empty of buildings

Holton Mill, just outside
Halesworth, is one of the
best-preserved windmills in
Adnams country.

until you reach St Andrew's Church; its size is a sign of what Walberswick used to be in the prosperous days when fishing and shipbuilding were profitable.

Like Blythburgh, Walberswick's population fell when its industry declined; then, maintaining the great fifteenth-century church became impossible. Much of it was abandoned, becoming a ruin. Within it the original south aisle became the parish church of today. Fortunately the fine 85ft tower with a battlemented parapet and the south porch have survived.

Just past the church, Palmers Lane leads down to the river. It is possible to drive part of the way the 'turn round' point being marked by a seat. A plaque and concrete base make it clear that this was the site of Walberswick Station on the old narrow gauge Halesworth to Southwold railway; passengers must have been prepared for a long walk to and from the village – or have been able to arrange wheeled transport.

If you are bound for the river, a straight mile along the old track bed leads to the Bailey Bridge, the modern replacement for the original railway bridge. Across the river is the Adnams' Harbour Inn, a pub with atmosphere, as they say. The fish and chip shops are a dream. If you plan to walk on to Southwold' it couldn't be simpler; continue along the track which leads directly to the site of the station.

On the way are fabulous views across the Common and reaching Southwold itself at the end of the track is the Adnams' Blyth (formerly Station) Hotel.

Walberswick Parish Church and the ruins show how big it once was.

If you decide to go the other way and into Walberswick there is another treat in store. The houses and gardens are a delight and there is, of course, The Adnams' Anchor Inn, modernised and extended, on the corner as the road turns left to the Green. Take your camera out here as greens like this one are rare indeed. There is refreshment here as well as a view; look for the home-made doughnuts which are not to be missed. Beyond the Green the road opens out and there are large car parks on the grass on both sides; here is the river mouth, fishermen's huts and a distant view of Southwold. A ferry for foot passengers only crosses here.

Walk, if you are so inclined, along the riverbank, or seawards crossing the little creek, now just a hint of the passage through Dunwich Harbour. From the little wooden bridge genera-tions of children have spent hours crabbing; continue along paths through clumps of sea grass, across patches of sand, then over a ridge on to the beach itself. Way to the south are the low cliffs of Dunwich and beyond them the outline of Sizewell Nuclear Power Station.

As you return to the parking area do not miss the Bell Inn on the left (Adnams again!). Parts of the building are 400 years old and the flagged floors, open fireplaces and low ceilings give it character. Like the Anchor, it is popular for its accommodation and its food.

The pub – and indeed the village – have had hauntings. One story is of the smell of burning when there were no bonfires and of strange appearances; once a mysterious stranger who was not there at all sat in the bar and another came and went past the church. He was seen by no other than an author who became famous: George Orwell.

Walberswick's attraction for painters is obvious: everything here speaks of an unchanging way of life. The sea and river always provided work: fishing and boat building kept the village alive, although danger was never far away. The riverbank was a work place, with tarred huts and fishermens's gear that gave the painters the scenery they loved. Then there was the weather, the majestic skies, changes of light on the water and the seashore itself.

The flowers that flourished in the sandy soil and the salt air were a fascination, as were the activities on the beach, especially the children at play: The Christchurch Mansion art collection in Ipswich includes paintings done at Walberswick by P. Wilson Steer; the remarkable Suffolk flower painting of Charles Rennie Mackintosh can be seen at the Hunterian Art Gallery, University of Glasgow. He was at Walberswick in 1914-15.

Adnams' pubs:

| Anchor Inn | The Street, Walberswick | 01502 722112 (Accomm) |
| Bell Inn | Ferry Road, Walberswick | 01502 723109 (Accomm) |

Dunwich

Generations of local families who kept holiday postcards will have a valuable record of the final years of Dunwich's last cliff-top church, All Saints. Each year more of it fell on to the beach as old postcards show, until the west tower collapsed in 1919.

It was one of eight in the glory days; St Felix settled there in AD 630 and became the first bishop of East Anglia. There is still in the Diocese of St Edmundsbury and Ipswich, a suffragan bishop of Dunwich.

Some of the early descriptions of Dunwich were fanciful. The town was said to have had 'fifty two churches and religious houses, a King's palace, a Bishop's seat and a Mint'. That it was important there is no doubt. Dunwich was second only to Ipswich in the county in terms of population according to the Domesday Book and in 1479 a battery was placed there, recorded as the first gun fortification on the Suffolk coast.

Today the old town is beneath the waves. The east coast of England has always been vulnerable to the sea; movement of the water is southerly and the main effect is to build up shingle banks in some places, while scouring takes place in others. Such a bank grew steadily just south of Southwold, protecting Dunwich and its harbour; sadly, that very growth was to spell doom for Dunwich.

Several times in the thirteenth century the harbour mouth became blocked and was laboriously reopened, but total disaster overtook the town in January 1328. A terrible storm and high tide destroyed the lower part of Dunwich and blocked the harbour mouth completely. Gone were the houses and workshops, finished was the shipbuilding that had been the mainstay of Dunwich. What the sea had left undone to the harbour, the Dunwich River continued to do, bringing its silt into what had been an important haven, but which gradually became choked up.

There were further storms and dreadful damage at regular intervals; the Market Place was inundated and in 1740 there was a final disaster.

The sea 'took its own' and in the process created a new river mouth to the north where the Blyth now meets the sea near Southwold. A view north beyond the Dunwich seashore car park shows the small river on its way to Walberswick across the marshes where part of the harbour will have been.

Once All Saints Church had gone over the cliff, little remained of old Dunwich, apart from some fragments of Greyfriars Priory and its gateway still standing by the roadside west of the cliff top.

Close to the nineteenth-century church of St James are the ruins of a Lepers' Chapel, the Leper Hospital of St James, built in about 1150. Only a small proportion of the building has survived; in its day it must have been very impressive. The apse has round-headed windows and elaborate arcading where there were once seats.

A buttress from the last church to go over the cliff in 1919 was recovered and stands forlornly in the south west corner of the churchyard.

There is more of interest to see at the Dunwich Museum close to the Ship Inn. Walk along the beach below the sandy cliffs (these are dangerous); who knows what you may find as the waves uncover the shingle.

Adnams' pubs:

White Horse	Darsham Road, Westleton	01728 648222 (Accomm)
Bell Inn	The Green, Middleton	01728 648286
Eel's Foot	Leiston Road, Eastbridge, Leiston	01728 830154 (Accomm)

Dunwich Priory Gateway is the sole reminder of an important town now lost to the sea.

The Leper Chapel's ruins in the present churchyard recall medieval support for the sick.

Halesworth and Walpole

Anyone with exploring in mind would do well to remember how important rivers have always been. None more so than the Blyth, which rises in central Suffolk; originally it reached the sea at Dunwich - that mysteriously disappeared port - once capital of East Anglia.

When the river was a commercial waterway it was used by the black-sailed wherries; bulk cargoes like coal came in and local agricultural produce moved down river.

West of Bythburgh, once the limit of navigation, estuary and marshes are left behind, replaced by water meadows and cultivated fields. Four locks on this stretch of the river made it navigable as far as Halesworth in 1756; the town had nine maltings in the 1800s and brewing was a major industry. Quay Street in the town is a reminder of river traffic; wherries like the Star of Halesworth were far more efficient than the traditional wagon and horses.

Halesworth's main shopping street, the Thoroughfare, now pedestrianised, has a bridge over the stream at its north end; the only movement there today comes from the ducks. Beyond, one road leads towards Southwold, the other (A144); going north is Stone Street, the Roman road that strikes out as straight as an arrow to Bungay.

But there is much more to Halesworth; at the upper end of the Thoroughfare just where you would expect, close to the church, is the Angel Hotel, one of Adnams' oldest houses. The first landlord there is recorded as John Pryme in 1584.

The Angel was always a vital part of Halesworth life, a coaching inn with extensive gardens to the rear and outbuildings such as stables and a maltings. The traditional stone–flagged courtyard where alighting coach passengers would have gone to find refreshment is now glass-roofed and is used as a lounge area. The array of bells that once summoned staff to deal with passengers' needs remains, as does the original tavern clock with its Oriental decoration. It was made in 1780 by George Suggate, a well known local clock maker.

Round the walls inside the Angel are notices of local 'happenings' like the launch of the first East Indiaman at the shipyard and the disappearance of an 'amateur' gentleman whose valuable belongings were left unclaimed. One suspects that he was carrying cash and that

Halesworth's Angel Hotel (Adnams) has retained its layout as a coaching inn.

this tempted some villain to steal it; if so, the gentleman's body seems not to have been discovered.

The Angel was always popular for wedding receptions. One story of long ago tells of a tragedy when a bride; still in her white wedding gown, fell over the balcony at the end of the courtyard to her death on the stone floor below. All the versions of the story say that it was an accident, although they disagree about the number of the bedroom she occupied; a girl in white is said to wander about still waiting for a call to her heavenly life.

The business life of Halesworth was closely linked to the Angel Hotel. It was a meeting place for local businessmen; matters of common interest such as opening up the river for trade, the extension of the East Suffolk railway to the town in the 1850s and – no doubt – the establishment of the Southwold branch line in 1879 were anxiously discussed.

One of Halesworth's best kept secrets can be found by going to the north side of St Mary's Church. Take Rectory Lane towards the river and you will see a fine example of a 'crinkle-crankle', serpentine or ribbon wall. These walls were a Dutch tradition, (see p. 82) and other examples of the Dutch connection will be illustrated elsewhere in this book.

Upstream from Halesworth the river and the B1117 road follow much the same course; Walpole is only a short distance and among the first buildings is one of the most historic in Suffolk. It stands on the right with fields opposite; plain within and without set behind iron railings, a few tombstones and a small notice board are the only clues that this was an old Meeting House of the Dissenters and used as a Congregational Chapel since 1647.

Search in vain for colour, decoration and an altar. It is the centrally placed pulpit with its handsome high sounding board that faces the visitor. Downstairs the furniture consists of box pews; if they look uninviting, the benches in the gallery must have been put together with whatever timber was at hand and look incredibly uncomfortable.

Next up river is Heveningham Hall, with its man-made lake. The eighteenth-century house was rebuilt for the Vanneck family, interiors by James Wyatt and grounds landscaped by Capability Brown. Sadly it is not open to the public, but there are distant views of the house from the roadside.

Walpole's Old Chapel near Halesworth is a rare example of a countryside meeting house in regular use today.

The Old Chapel's Pulpit can best be seen from the gallery.

Adnams' pubs:

Queen's Head	The Street, Bramfield	01986 784214
Angel Hotel	The Thoroughfare, Halesworth	01986 873365 (Accomm)
White Hart	The Thoroughfare, Halesworth	01986 873386

Sibton Abbey

Unless you are watchful you may miss the abbey altogether. That would be a great pity, as it was the only Cistercian house in Suffolk. The overgrown ruins stand across the fields from St Mary's Church on the A1120 Stowmarket to Yoxford Tourist Route about halfway between Peasenhall and Yoxford.

Although a small abbey with an abbot and twelve monks and founded in 1149, it had many donors and was prosperous. Like other Cistercian abbeys its site was isolated; here it is in the water meadows of the little Yox River.

Look for a footpath sign in the hedgerow just east of St Mary's Church at Sibton, climb the stile and follow the field edge north to the little wooden river bridge. Go through the metal gate and cross, then left along the bank and through a gap into the next field. The abbey ruins are about 50yds away on the right.

Sibton on the River Yox had
a small priory. The village sign
shows two white-robed monks
with a sheep from their large
flock.

The priory's ruins can best be seen when foliage is not thick.

Tall round-arched windows of the refectory are well visible, but tree and bushes, especially in summer hide much else, other than an eastern Norman arch. Just to the southeast are the remains of the abbey fishpond now massed with water irises. At the end of a dry spring in 2007 there was just a small pool of water in the deepest part of the pond, otherwise it was merely damp.

Allow twenty minutes each way (more if it is muddy where tractors turn at the field gap). Cars can be parked by the church gate. The village sign there shows monks with a sheep.

Adnams' pubs:

| Kings Head | Gorams Mill Lane, Laxfield | 01986 798395 (Accomm) |
| White Horse | Woodbridge Road, Badingham | 01728 638280 |

Laxfield

The Suffolk rivers Blyth, Aide and Deben all rise in a comparatively high part of the county. It certainly feels like it following the rivers upstream and at Laxfield, almost in the middle of Suffolk is the source of the Blyth.

Where is the village to be found then, what else is there to explore? Framlingham, Eye, or even over the county border at Diss; but Laxfield is so worth a visit on its own account.

All Saints Church: visitors here may see the resemblance of the impressive 100ft tower to that at Eye with its extensive use of flushwork as well as of costly freestone.

The nave of about 1400 is 36ft wide, making the church very spacious. Hammer beams in the roof are concealed by coving as at Framlingham and there are examples of rich carving. The sixteenth-century benches are richly carved and there are some fine poppy heads.

The 'Seven Sacrament' font is one of the finest remaining. Instead of a shaft it has a series of steps, the top consisting of four places for the priest and godparents. The seven sacraments are carved round the font with the Baptism of Jesus on the bowl.

Also close to the river is Sibton White Horse, an outstanding inn in the area.

Laxfield Parish Church has
many visitors; its font is superb.

A church at Laxfield was mentioned in Domesday; no doubt there was an earlier one in Saxon times.

The Guildhall: donated by the Lord of the Manor in 1461, the Guildhall of St Mary was intended as a Church House for the use of village religious and charitable guilds. The timber framing and brick nogging make it conspicuous opposite the church.

The museum, which occupies the upper floor, was founded in 1968 and is governed by a trust.

A special room at the museum has been allocated displays of fashion and costume as well as shoes. The main display area is taken up with items of local industry such as milling, farming and crafts. A feature commemorates the death of John Noyes, a village shoemaker whose Puritan beliefs resulted in his being burned at the stake in 1577. He was brought to his own village for this to give a message to everyone.

The Kings Head (Low House): this pub has had so many superlatives: 'unique', 'an undoubted classic' and 'one of Suffolk's classics' that it deserves more than usual space. It takes it name from its position at the lower part of the village.

Some 600 years old, thatched, with plaster walls, this has to be seen to be believed. It was named for King Henry VIII, as in the twenty-eighth year of his reign he granted the Manor of Laxfield to Edmund Bedingfield. The first tenant of the pub was listed in 1700, but few records of tenancies exist earlier than the eighteenth and nineteenth centuries because properties in

Laxfield's Guildhall, facing the church, houses a fine museum.

King's Head (Low House) at Laxfield is one of Adnams' best-known village pubs and has changed little: there is no bar!

The King's Head Servery takes orders and passes them to regulars in the 'family room'.

the manor were 'copyholds'. In the early years it brewed its own beer and was a house where local farming business was done.

The main public room is entered from the front door; the open fire and old oven once used to roast meat gave its name 'the Kitchen', where regulars could sit on the high-backed settles round the fire playing pub games such as dominoes. Don't look for the bar – there isn't one! Drinks are served straight from the casks in the taproom at the back, all by gravity, and brought to the Kitchen. There are two smaller rooms and a recent extension providing a formal restaurant.

The pub has been untouched by juke boxes and space invader games; tradition is big at Low House. It is said that visitors used to be puzzled by a cry from the staff 'Who's for Ipswich?' This was a customary way of collecting orders for Ipswich almond pudding.

Do not leave Laxfield without visiting the church, the Guildhall and Low House, which is one of Adnams' best.

The pub gardens are beautiful and there is a holiday flat to let at Low House too!

Directions:

A12 to Yoxford then
A1120 west (tourist route)
At Dennington turn right on to the B1116 for Laxfield

7

Historic and Other Features

Haddiscoe, Harringfleet, St Olaves and Fritton Lake

This is exploring with a difference. If you enjoy waterways, marshes, mills and riverside villages, then spend a day along the lower Waveney Valley. Nothing less than a whole day will be enough and the recommended route is vital if nothing is to be missed.

You will be making first for Haddiscoe on the Norfolk side of the Waveney, then St Olaves, Herringfleet and Fritton Lake on the Suffolk bank. Haddiscoe has a rail station on the line from Norwich to Lowestoft; there used to be another one there on the former Beccles to Yarmouth Southtown route, sadly closed.

The Waveney does not reach the sea at Lowestoft as it seems to intend, but as your map will show turns northwards, wanders rather aimlessly, then joins the Yare at Breydon Water before both rivers flow into Yarmouth harbour and into the sea.

In 1832 a 2½ mile canal, the New Cut, was cut to connect the Waveney at St Olaves with the Yare at Reedham. It provided for the first time a direct river route between Norwich and Lowestoft through Oulton Dyke and Oulton Broad, then via Mutford Lock into Lowestoft harbour; sad to say it was not a financial success, but is popular with today's boaters.

To enjoy the whole of the itinerary try one of the following routes for Haddiscoe:

From Bungay A143
From Beccles A146/143
From Norwich A146
Fork left on B1136 at Hales

On the left do not miss Haddiscoe's lovely round towered church of St Mary; there are many with round towers in this area and that at Haddiscoe has an unusual chequered band of flushwork round the top. The A143 passes across the winding, tree-fringed Haddiscoe 'dam' with marshes on both sides, then crosses the railway line. Immediately afterwards are two bridges, one over the New Cut and the other over the Waveney with wonderful views from both.

That over the river is St Olaves' bridge and in the distance is the Priory Wind Pump on the right bank of the river.

St Olaves Priory: it was founded by the Augustinians in about 1216; it was never large, having had only seven canons besides the prior. At the Dissolution in 1537 it passed into the ownership of Sir Henry Jerningham. He converted part of the priory into a private house using materials from the ruins; more may well have been used for the nineteenth-century restoration of Herringfleet Church.

The priory was made of flint, much of it now only visible as foundations. The cloisters, 68ft sq., can still be seen, also the vaulted undercroft of the refectory; against its north face is a partly ruined brick wall, probably of Jerningham's house.

Herringfleet Wind Pump: a turning off the A143 near the Priory marked B1074, Herringfleet and Blundeston, leads to a Broads Authority car park on the right called Herringfleet Hills, a mile or so away.

Leisure craft at St Olaves illustrate the Waveney's popularity.

St Olaves' Priory was always small, but its remains are well cared for.

A plan of the walks from here is displayed; for the wind pump make for the trees at 'ten o'clock', follow the footpath and steps down to a bridle way marked with blue signs and go through a gate to the marsh. Along the footpath there are stiles to be climb and possible muddy patches, but the wind pump is visible all the way from the edge of the marsh.

A footbridge leads to the mill itself; built about 1820 it is the last remaining old style Broadland Wind Pump of the smock mill type. Octagonal and wooden framed, it has four cloth-spread sails and a tail pole and winch for winding the cap into the wind. Its work was to lift water from the marsh into the river using an external 16ft scoop wheel; it continued working until the 1950s.

Herringfleet Wind Pump is preserved in working order by Suffolk County Council and is demonstrated on some Sundays. For details call 01473 264755. Behind the wind pump and above the raised bank of the river you will see the diesel units of the railway passing back and forth between Norwich and Lowestoft.

Fritton Lake is part of the Somerleyton estate and is only a mile or so from St Olaves on the A143. Now a country park, the lake is nearly three miles long and was a result of the flooding of former peat diggings, which as we now know, was also the origin of the Norfolk Broads. Peat excavating, or 'turbary' was a valuable means of obtaining fuel and was common practice in the twelfth and thirteenth centuries. On the low-lying marshland flooding must have taken place rapidly, especially when channels had been cut to the rivers to ship out and market peat elsewhere.

Curved and fringed by trees and reed beds, Fritton Lake has become something of a holiday paradise. In its early days as a Country Park, Fritton's main activities were boating and fishing for day visitors; today, woodland lodges and estate cottages are available as holiday 'lets' or to buy. The Fritton House Hotel provides high-class meals and guests can play golf, wind surf, sail and go horse riding.

There are plenty of activities for children on land and water; for older visitors looking for something less strenuous there is a putting course and formal gardens to enjoy. Food is no problem; take a picnic or have a meal in the restaurant at the visitor centre.

Fritton Lake is part of the Somerleyton estate and is now a popular visitor and holiday venue.

Fritton Lake's 'Decoy' was once a valuable earner.

A generation or so ago the Country Park was known as Fritton Decoy because netting wild fowl was a profitable business there for 300 years. It was done using a netted tunnel, attracting wild ducks into the tunnel following tame ones lured with grain, or enticed into following the decoy man's dog. Once in the tunnel and the trap at the end there was no escape.

There was a ready market for wild duck for the table and a number of decoys on large estates made money for their owners.

Take a trip on Fritton Lake and ask the boatman to show you the mouth of the decoy.

Fritton Lake's opening days and hours call 01473 488288.

Adnams' pubs:

Fleece Inn	St Mary's Street, Bungay	01986 892192
Butchers Arms	London Road, Beccles	01502 712243
Wherry Inn	7 The Street, Geldeston, Beccles	01508 518371

Minsmere Nature Reserve (RSPB)

The coastline of Suffolk richly deserves its designation as an Area of Outstanding Natural Beauty; within it are five wildlife reserves. The northernmost is Dingle Marshes north of Dunwich; the southernmost is Boyton Marshes on the west bank of the Butley River close to Orford.

Minsmere is one of the RSPB's 'flagship' reserves, having begun life in 1947 through a leasing agreement, followed thirty years later when the 1,500 acre area was bought; since then more land has been added, including the Levels, where the original Leiston Abbey was built in 1182.

Set in a stretch of sandy coastal heath-land known as the Sandlings, Minsmere now has fresh-water reed beds, saltwater lagoons such as the Scrape, sand dunes and shingle. The whole area

Lagoon at Minsmere RSPB site.

is 'managed' to provide habitats for a wide variety of wild life: reeds are cut to benefit bitterns, marsh harriers and bearded tits, while water levels in the Scrape are controlled for nesting birds in the spring, waders in the summer and ducks, geese and swans in the winter.

It was the rumoured reappearance of breeding avocets at Minsmere in 1947 after 100 years that created great interest; the creation of shallow lagoons to provide good nesting conditions at Minsmere and new nesting areas at Havergate Island further south (see p. 131) secured the future of the avocet colonies.

The success with avocets was accompanied by the safeguarding of other endangered species such as marsh harriers and bitterns.

There are two nature trails at Minsmere, each about 1½ miles long; it takes some two hours to walk either of these. On my first visit I took the trail south and west to watch at the Bittern Hide and the Island Mere Hide about ½ mile further before turning back towards the Visitor Centre. Next time I went east towards the sea shore, followed closely as I passed the pond (the old car park) by inquisitive family groups of sand martins that nest in the sand cliff there.

High up and away to the left are the Coastguard Cottages in the care of The National Trust, part of their 'Coastal Centre and Beach'. A specially designed walk (about two hours) from the car park there follows public footpaths round the perimeter of the RSPB site into Eastbridge and to Adnams' Eel's Foot Inn. This pub is 600 years old and retains many of its traditions, including the Eel's Foot Singers, who do a programme of folk songs there on Thursday evenings.

The pub has been modernised and there are now en-suite bedrooms. Try it and you will be comfortable and very well fed. Turn left out of the pub and walk down to Minsmere Sluice; left again along the dunes path will take you back to the Coastguard Cottages. Most of the Minsmere Reserve is accessible to wheelchairs and seven bird watching hides take visitors close to wild life activities.

Well over 300 different species of birds, 1,000 species of moths, thirty-three species of butterflies and twenty-three species of dragonflies have been recorded at Minsmere. In the reed beds are flourishing populations of otters and water voles.

Because of the changing wild life population at Minsmere and the different breeding times, there is always something new to see. An excellent visitor centre includes an information desk and a hiring service of binoculars; the shop has a tea room next door providing light meals. Parking and toilets are close by.

Directions:

Minsmere: From A12 follow brown tourist signs posted as follows:
South of Blythburgh and north of Yoxford
Both routes are via Westleton

Adnams' pubs:

Eel's Foot	Leiston Road, Eastbridge	01728 830154
White Horse	Darsham Road, Westleton	01728 648222

Havergate Island Nature Reserve RSPB

Now uninhabited and the only island in Suffolk, Havergate is a twenty-minute boat trip south from Orford Quay along the narrow neck of Orfordness towards the river mouth.

It was the action of water that created the island by depositing sand and mud over many hundreds of years. Although always in danger of flooding, protective banks were built round Havergate as long as 500 years ago and farmers began to improve the soil, grow crops and bring cattle from the mainland to graze there.

Summer grazing continued until the Second World War, but neglect during wartime brought flooding and grazing ended. The lonely island became a breeding ground for many species of birds.

The first avocets to breed in Britain were reported there in 1947 and the RSPB bought the island in 1948. It has become a habitat for twenty-five to thirty species of waders, ducks and geese, including about 100 pairs of avocets.

A good time to go is between April and the end of August when the reserve is open on the first and third weekends of the month and every Thursday. The boat leaves Orford Quay at 10.00 a.m. and returns at 3.00 p.m. Bookings have to be made through RSPB at Minsmere (01728 648281) and visitors are set down at a landing stage near the Visitor Centre where there is a hide overlooking the Main Lagoon.

Suitable clothing and footwear are recommended and a picnic lunch should be taken; a picnic site is available, also toilets. In the case of bad weather there is good shelter at the centre where information material is kept and the hide provides bird watchers with the opportunity they seek. An RSPB volunteer guide joins each boat party.

Two of the five hides on the island are to the north of the centre, overlooking the Gullery and the North Lagoon. Beyond the Main Lagoon to the south are Belper's Lagoon and, after crossing a shingle bank, Dovey's Lagoon at the end of the island.

Each lagoon on the island has a hide and there is also a cottage flood viewpoint; all are reached by well-marked footpaths and bridges to the entrances.

Visits in July and August allow visitors to see growing chicks feeding, waders are migrating southwards and becoming neighbours of the families of avocets; even little egrets and spoonbills may be seen at that time. Redshanks are regular breeders at Havergate.

Black headed gulls are the most numerous on the island, always on the move and calling loudly. But it is the avocets which command much interest, also brown hares, a colony of about fifty in number, which surprise visitors lucky enough to see them. On the unusual conditions at Havergate that include salt marsh, shingle, salt-water lagoons and mudflats are many interesting plant species including gorse, grasses, sea campion and yellow vetch. But for real intense colour go in August when the sea lavender is in full bloom: you will never forget the carpet of purple – or the avocets.

Directions:

Orford: A12 to Woodbridge, then A1152 via Melton
Fork right on B1084 via Butley
Good, convenient parking near Orford Quay
Excellent tea shop on the Quay (Open 'all hours')

Adnams' pubs:

The King's Head	Orford	01394 450271 (Accomm)
Jolly Sailor	Quay Street, Orford	01394 450243
Oyster Inn	Woodbridge Road, Butley	01394 450790

Parham Moat Hall

It is remarkable that so many buildings in the Suffolk countryside are, or have been moated –
more than 500 of them. Some moats, it is true, are more statements of importance by
landowning families than to fulfil a useful purpose. Yet they did provide protection: the drawbridge at Helmingham Hall is raised and lowered night and morning even today.

Most of the Suffolk moats were at manor houses, halls, or isolated farm houses called by the
village name with the addition 'Moat Farm'. The heavy Suffolk clay was certainly suitable for
maintaining water levels in moats and provided building material when dug out; when fresh
water could flow into moats from springs, a secure water supply became available and fish
could be bred for food.

In early days, though, moats were a defence, especially for houses in isolated positions like
Moat Hall, Parham, well out of the village and approached from an even smaller settlement,
Silverlace Green. Today the approach lane passes a line of smaller farm buildings (Moat Farm),
before reaching a brick gateway and a private garden; the wing of the house from here is half
timbered – interesting, but not exceptional.

But going through a field gate and following a public footpath to the north east there is
something rare and beautiful: a brick mansion rising sheer out of the moat. It shows its age,
having been built about 1500, or even earlier, by the Willoughby family. The two bays and
chimney stack surely lack another bay and chimney to the south east, where there are foundations of the missing part.

The windows, two lights on the lower floor and three lights with transoms above are remarkable
in themselves; on the bays and chimney the fine brickwork is decorated with Tudor diaper patterns.

Visit Parham when you go to Framlingham and you will have a unique experience.

Parham Moat Hall directions:

From Framlingham take B1116 Woodbridge Road
At Parham village turn left, the Street and Hall Road
Continue uphill past Silverlace Farm to a sharp bend
Turn on to track marked Moat Farm and park near farm buildings
Walk down to gateway and footpath

Adnams' pubs:

| Railway Inn | Station Road, Framlingham | 01728 723693 |
| Queens Head | The Street, Brandeston | 01728 685307 |

Parham Moat Hall is a splendid example of
Suffolk's many moated halls.

Ipswich and the Orwell Cruise

Without the Orwell, Ipswich might never have been, or at least not until very much later.
There is good evidence to show that there was a settlement around AD 600 on the north bank
of the Orwell, one of several along the rivers of Suffolk such as the Deben and Alde.

At Gipeswic (the name is derived from the River Gipping that becomes the Orwell at
Ipswich), the ford near today's Stoke Bridge was an attraction for early settlers. 'Stoke' refers to
a holy place: Stoke by Nayland is an example, and a burial ground has been uncovered. Other
finds confirm international trade was being carried out through the use of the river.

Such was the growth of the town even before Norwich was founded that Ipswich as it
now is soon began importing wine and millstones and exporting wool and textiles to western
Europe. A pottery industry making Ipswich Ware became of great importance; down river
products were sent to London and all parts of England. No doubt a route upstream along the
Gipping also became an avenue for trade and attracted new Anglo- Saxon settlements.

Since those early days quays and docks were built to serve local industry and to provide
berths for larger and larger vessels. The Orwell was widened and deepened and the Wet Dock
was built in 1842; whatever the state of the tide the lock gates ensured deep water for the
movement of ships. The handsome, pillared Old Custom House has the offices of the Port
Authority that regulates river traffic today.

The best way to appreciate and enjoy the Orwell is to take a cruise to Felixstowe, Harwich
and back. With a seating capacity of 118 for day trips and two decks, 'Orwell Lady' is operated
by Orwell River Cruises Ltd, starting and finishing at the Wet Dock.

Details and booking at Ipswich Tourist Information Centre: 01473 258070

Leaving the Wet Dock once water levels permit, the outline of the Orwell Bridge shows up
sharp against the sky. It took three years to build and carries the A14 and A12 traffic away from

Orwell Bridge.

The terminal accommodates enormous container ships; these can be seen at close quarters from the Orwell river cruise vessels.

Orwell river cruise.
(Courtesy of Ipswich
Borough Council)

the congested local roads. Its total length is 1,287m with an air draft of 43m. To watch another vessel passing beneath the main arch is to realise what a huge structure this is; another revelation is the graceful curve along its length when passing beneath it.

Most of the countryside features are on the right bank going out, like farms and cottages; one unusual building is the red-brick Freston Tower standing six storeys high and with one room on each floor. Although many believe it was built as a lookout, a more charming explanation is that the owner had it built as a place of study for his daughter. This version has each storey being used for different and successive periods of study each day.

The moorings at Woolverstone Marina and the many yachts tied up there mark the Royal Harwich Yacht Club close by. Next to the club house is a white-painted cottage 'Cat House'; this became notorious during seventeenth century smuggling days, when the owners used to put their stuffed white cat in the window when there were no Excise men on watch.

The eighteenth-century Orwell Park House on the opposite bank was the home of Admiral Vernon who was Admiral of the Fleet and became known as Old Grog after ordering the watering down of naval rum, the traditional grog.

The best known feature on this stretch of the river is Pin Mill with its famous Butt & Oyster pub right on the edge of the water. Commercial barges used to be built here and operated from the deep water; many have been restored and take part in an annual race. But the river is full today with pleasure craft. The Cliff Plantation along the riverbank is in the care of The National Trust and has marked footpaths. Try the fish at the Butt & Oyster and the beer by Adnams. The pub interior has its original tiled floor, settles, benches and old signs – an atmosphere all of its own.

Levington and Trimley Beach are on the opposite shore. By now the cranes of the Port of Felixstowe are in sight. Passing alongside the enormous container ships with their stacks of containers reaching ever upwards, it is difficult to imagine that there are more below than there are visible. How those giants could ever stop in an emergency with the weight they carry is a mystery.

Trinity Terminal is now the country's largest container quay, stretching 2,354m; it can accommodate the biggest ships afloat today. In 2007 the Port celebrated a record number of containers being handled on a single vessel: 5,586 in March. The vessel was the China Shipping Container Line's 'America' and the company plans even larger ships; there are plans, too, for a second container terminal to be built.

Passing the Port of Harwich where the River Stour meets the Orwell estuary, Shotley Gate is to the north and in the waterway are lightships at anchor. Once common round the coasts they are now rarely seen. Passing close to the former HMS Ganges, the naval training establishment, Orwell Lady's return journey begins, a total 3½ hour cruise.

Directions:

Ipswich Wet Dock:

From A14 junction 55 (also A12 junction take A1214)
Turn right on to A137, follow to Bridge Street
Cross river, turn right and follow one-way system
Turn into Star Lane
Right at roundabout into Duke Street and car park for Wet Dock
or
A14 junction 56, the A137, under railway bridge
Continue to cross river at Stoke Bridge
Continue as above

Hollesley Bay and Shingle Street

As far back as 1500 a number of Suffolk's coastal areas were identified as the most likely to be attacked by invaders. In addition to Harwich Haven, a good anchorage off-shore and a suitable beach for a landing were to be found at Lowestoft, Sole Bay (Southwold) and Hollesley Bay (pronounced Hosely). For those reasons, a defence against Napoleon was concentrated along that coast by the building of Martello Towers; examples can be seen from Aldeburgh southwards. During the Second World War anti-tank defences were set up behind the shore, together with pill boxes and gun batteries.

An added advantage for an intended invader is a lonely shore and an empty 'hinterland': this is certainly a good description of Hollesley Bay and Shingle Street. Go east beyond Hollesley village and you see for yourself; once there was a 'colony' at Hollesley, now called a young offenders' institution, but beyond here is the shore itself. Shingle Street is a strong candidate for the loneliest, coldest, windiest place in the county, perhaps this side of the Arctic Circle. It is the sort of place where your week's wash always hangs out horizontally, where looking out of your ground floor window you can see nothing but the bank of shingle, which is the only protection you have from the sea.

Although there are a few houses just behind the shingle bank mainly owned by summer visitors today, you have to ask why anyone would want to live there. How long can a settlement here last, given the action of the sea and the movement of the shingle bank? Its history only goes back to the building of the Martello Towers around 1810; there are four in the few miles between here and Bawdsey to the south. Fishing has been the only occupation – and that from the beach.

The lack of shelter from the wind discourages gardeners; trees suffer particularly badly and the shingle-covered surface of the foreshore has little to show apart from low-growing

Shingle Street and Hollesley Bay are the loneliest area of the Suffolk coast.

plants like Sea Bindweed, Yellow Horned Poppy and a variety of grasses that can stand the salt air.

A walk northwards from the white coastguard station will take you to the mouth of the River Ore. You will be on your own on the endless bank of shingle apart from sea birds; their cries, the wind and the waves on the shore the only sounds you will hear. Low tides expose islands at the Ore's mouth; further upstream beyond the Butley River and Orford its name becomes the Alde. Following its course to seaward is the extraordinary shingle spit reaching Orford Ness, then Aldeburgh.

A visit to Shingle Street is an experience. It is less of a place than a 'happening', so the journey there from Woodbridge across heathland and through the unusual 'Sandling' country has to be savoured and cherished.

Directions:

Hollesley Bay and Shingle Street:

A12 to Woodbridge, then A1152, crossing Wilford Bridge
Fork right, B1083 and pass Sutton Hoo
At Bromeswell fork left for Hollesley
Cross Sutton Heath and pass RAF Woodbridge (forested area)
Follow Shingle Street signs
At Duck Corner forward past T sign
In 1 mile, cross bridge, marshy pools on either side
Continue to white block (coastguard station)
Car Park (shingle surface) — road only serves houses further.

Adnams' pubs: see Woodbridge

Hoxne and St Edmund

There can be few historical accounts that have made such a deep and lasting impression as the murder of King Edmund by the Danes in 870.

Witness the number of churches in Suffolk like that at Southwold dedicated to Edmund, carvings such as that at Hadleigh showing the murdered King's head, or medieval stained glass repeating the story. Some of the finest glass in the county is at Holy Trinity Church, Long Melford; in the east window there, below our Lady of Pity is King Edmund, crowned, with the Abbot of Bury kneeling below him.

See Bures (p. 137) for the story of his crowning and Bury St Edmunds (p. 14) dealing with his shrine. Accounts of his death at the hands of the Danes, chiefly the 'where' and 'how', vary. The version most strongly held is that he was taken at Hoxne by the Danes, whose invading army overwhelmed that of the Saxons. One account speaks of Edmund's surrender; another that he was betrayed whilst on the run which appeals to me.

Hiding under a bridge over a stream at Hoxne (pronounced Hoxen) he was seen by a young couple on their way to be married at the village church. Under threat from the Danes they pointed to the reflection of Edmund's gold spurs in the water. Once a prisoner, his life would have been spared if he had renounced his Christianity; this he refused to do and was tied to a tree and killed with many arrows. His head was cut off and thrown into the bushes.

The king's followers came later and found his body, but not his head until their attraction was drawn by the cries of a wolf calling 'Here, Here' and holding the king's head in its mouth. This is the image which endures to this day, deeply engrained in local belief: so much so that crossing the bridge on the way to a marriage service in the church is held to be bad luck.

Goldbrook Bridge (rebuilt several times) is still there by the Hoxne Community Centre where you can park your car. Up in the gable of the centre is a stone illustration of the King's capture in AD870: a short walk up the road past the cottages will take you to a monument where his murder took place. Keep to the pavement and follow it on to a raised footpath clear of the traffic. A public footpath sign marks the edge of the field where the striking monument to the King's murder stands.

Once a wooded area, the horizon is now clear and the monument stands out conspicuously. Hoxne is a village of modest size; the church is at the upper end of the green, the Swan pub at the lower end. Just below the Swan is a road junction: turn left and Goldbrook Bridge is only a few yards along. Its date stone says 1878 – just about 1,000 years since Edmund was captured below.

The Anglo-Saxons raised a shrine over the grave of their king; his body was moved in 903 to a new and grander shrine at Beodricsworth, later to take the name Saint Edmundsbury and Edmund to be given the title King and Martyr.

Directions:

Al to A140 north and on to Scole roundabout
Close to roundabout take B1118 to Hoxne
Alternatively take A143 east and turn right near
Billingford (Note windmill there)

Adnams' pubs:

| Cherry Tree | 74 London Road, Harleston | 01379 852345 |
| Cardinal's Hat | Thoroughfare, Harleston | 01379 853748 |

8

Lost Branch Railway Lines

The Southwold Railway

Holidaymakers of the early 1930s on their way to Great Yarmouth or Lowestoft might well have wondered when their train stopped at Halesworth if carriages standing on a track beyond the up platform were part of a 'real' railway. Small, like something from a 'toytown' scene, they were what remained of a Southwold railway that used a separate platform at Halesworth. It ran the 8¾ miles to and from Southwold from September 1879 to April 1929. By 1882 there were three intermediate stations; Wenhaston, Blythburgh and Walberswick.

At the outset the railway was planned to be built with a narrow gauge track (3ft was chosen) on grounds of financial savings, both in its building and its operating. It was to be a 'light' railway with a single track; although this simplified the signalling system, speed was restricted to 16 mph and goods and passengers had to be transhipped at Halesworth – a time-consuming business.

Trains on the line usually consisted of two or three passenger coaches that had end doors and bench seats along the sides just like city trams; there was a van for passengers' luggage and seven or so varied goods wagons. Apart from the mail, fish and other local produce went out from Southwold and the country stations; coal and other basic goods and food was brought in via Halesworth.

There were four trains a day with extra goods-only services; at Blythburgh station a loop line was opened to allow trains to pass there. The three locomotives were specially built at Manchester; side tanks capable of coping with the unusual conditions.

After a slow start, the line's income improved sufficiently for a plan to convert the line to standard gauge to be considered and for a branch line to the harbour to be built. The latter was thought to be needful to support the Southwold fisheries, but by the time it had been built in 1914 the First World War had broken out; afterwards there was virtually no fishing industry to support.

In spite of the failure of the harbour branch enterprise, the railway was a great success in opening up Southwold as a holiday resort and encouraged house building in the town. Its future was assured.

From 1926 the railway started to lose money as road transport developed; passenger traffic went increasingly to buses which could be boarded in town and village centres. The scenic journey the railway offered could never compensate for the remoteness of Walberswick station; for example.

The set of humorous postcards produced by Reg Carter picturing some of the imagined events on the Southwold Railway is still in demand and can be bought at the railway shop, staffed by volunteers at No. 27 High Street, Southwold. In March 2007 the Railway Trust submitted a planning application to restore the railway.

Adnams' pubs: see Southwold

The Aldeburgh Branch

The Aldeburgh Branch is remembered with affection by hundreds of former pupils of Leiston Grammar School who boarded at Saxmundham in pre-war days for the 8.08 a.m. departure

Southwold Railway's gleaming loco about to leave for Halesworth.

and returned at 4.23 p.m. They filled the usual two coaches, many having arrived each morning at Saxmundham from Woodbridge, Melton and Wickham Market by a main line train that had picked up pupils from the Framlingham branch at Wickham Market on its way. Some even cycled to Saxmundham from villages such as Peasenhall.

Traffic was busy when the down train on the main line arrived; the Aldeburgh branch stood waiting on the up line until the main line train had gone before backing on to the platform where the waiting passengers stood.

Once away the Leiston and Aldeburgh branch train made for the junction signal box where driver or fireman collected the staff from the signalman while on the move, before going on to the single track of the Aldeburgh line.

Tackling the gradient climbing up to Clay Hills away from the junction was always hard work; on quiet mornings the sound of the steam locomotive labouring here could be heard from far away. Sometimes there were members of the public on the early morning train, but it was almost a 'school' train.

The line opened in 1859 and, after wartime restrictions, finally closed to passengers in 1966. It was pressure from Richard Garrett who owned the agricultural engineering company at Leiston: Leiston 'works', that resulted in the construction of the first section of the line to Leiston. This became busy and Leiston station handled a great deal of freight business.

Soon afterwards an extension to Aldeburgh was completed, where a train service was hoped to help the town to become a prosperous seaside resort. The station was very impressive, but was inconveniently located some way from the town and the sea front.

Passenger traffic failed to meet expectations although goods traffic, particularly the transport of local fresh fish, was promising.

One of several attempts to encourage travel on the line was the opening of a halt at Thorpeness, where a seaside village had been established by Glencairn Stuart Ogilvie. He had a shallow lake called the Mere dug close to the beach, then surrounded it with black and white timbered houses; a brick-built club, a pub and a golf course kept adults well occupied, while for children there was boating on the Mere, fishing from the banks and the seashore for bathing.

Present-day diesel unit at Saxmundham bound for Ipswich.

Aldeburgh branch train about to leave for Saxmundham.

Thorpeness needed a water supply: Ogilvie disguised his water tower by boarding it in and by creating a make-believe house on top, complete with windows and a tiled roof. It soon became known as the House in the Clouds: the make-believe has been converted into a real house and is let as holiday accommodation. Close by is a white windmill, originally from Aldringham, the next village, brought to Thorpeness and re-erected to add to the illusion of a village.

Like the station at Aldeburgh, Thorpeness Halt was too far from the beach to bring many passengers; they had a wearying walk on a narrow road and a long wait if they missed the train home. Arrangements on the platform were rather rustic; the 'buildings', including the ticket office were old, disused railway coaches and there was one open shelter.

Both Aldeburgh station and Thorpeness Halt have disappeared entirely, being replaced by modern houses. The track was lifted long ago, apart from the length from Saxmundham to a siding just east of Leiston station; this was used extensively for Sizewell Nuclear Power Station and remains available for current and future use.

The railway station buildings at Leiston have been converted into residential properties, but the platform itself and the crossing gates are much as the former school passengers would remember the scene.

There have been changes, of course: diesel units replaced steam locomotives and Garrett's Leiston Works closed. No longer does the Leiston 'Bull' sound at midday and at the beginning and end of the working shift.

Adnams' pubs:

Eel's Foot Inn	Eastbridge	01728 830154 (Accomm)
Engineers Arms	Main Street, Leiston	01728 830660

The Framlingham Branch

About six miles along, the only stops on the route were at Marlesford where the line crossed the A12 and at Parham, although in 1920 Hacheston Halt was added. Apart from a main line connection at Wickham Market (its station at Campsea Ashe was 2 miles from the village itself) there was little chance of attracting substantial passenger traffic other than excursions at week-ends in the summer to places like Felixstowe. It was from transport of freight such as coal, grain and cattle that most of the railway's revenue came.

The branch line would not have been built at all but for pressure from business men who could see the great advantages the railway would bring to Framlingham; true enough, the town did have a period of prosperity following its opening. There was a demand for land for the track of course, and the building of the line itself; businesses were attracted to sites close to the stations at Framlingham, Parham and Marlesford. At Framlingham the area close to the terminus along the line became a growing industrial and residential suburb; the Station Hotel with stables was an important addition.

The train service, steam hauled throughout, began with four trains each way per day, later increased to six. Most were mixed passenger and goods and it was always a slow journey: a number of level crossing gates had to be operated by locomotive men and there were several speed restrictions on the line.

Passengers at Hacheston Halt had to board or alight using a special car that was provided with retractable steps, as the so-called platform was at rail level. This was ideal material for schoolboy jokes in the area.

The train service did not last: competition from developing road transport was to sound its death knell, although some local critics held that business declined because the terminus was badly sited.

Framlingham Station building, now a shop.

Wartime needs brought some traffic to the line, but its closure to passenger services inevitably came in 1952. A curious survival until 1958 was the provision of a special train for students of Framlingham College at the beginning and end of terms; the freight service closed in 1965 and was the end of the railway era for Framlingham.

As elsewhere, disused railway buildings were put to residential or business use: at Framlingham the station building is now a centre for motorcycle sales. A variety of agricultural firms occupy other buildings on the site and the former goods shed remains.

The Station Hotel is next door and two or three minutes' walk towards town is Adnams' Railway Inn, with bar, snug and outdoor seating. A number of humorous notices are painted on the ceilings, one being 'Binder twine 2/- a reel'. Unless you are of a certain age and from the country you will not know how important this used to be in the days before combine harvesters. In their day binders would not only cut a cereal crop, but bind it into sheaves as well, hence binder twine.

Adnams' pubs:

The Railway Inn   9 Station Road, Framlingham   01728 723693

Hadleigh Branch

Bentley station just south of Ipswich on the main line to London was never much more than a wayside stop, but was useful as the nearest and most convenient point for a railway junction to serve Hadleigh, 7¼ miles away.

There were ambitious plans for the line to reach Lavenham and beyond, but the single track only ever extended to Hadleigh. The first passenger train ran in 1847, although freight traffic proved to be the mainstay of the line; the junction at Bentley was designed to handle trains to and from the London direction.

A short distance west of Bentley the line passed Capel St Mary and crossed the A12 at Capel Station – an impossibility today, bearing in mind the weight of modern road traffic.

Between the former railway track and Capel St Mary is Little Wenham, a small village as its name suggests. One of the oldest manor houses in the country is there: Little Wenham Hall, built in 1270. Privately owned and empty, it has architectural importance because apart from some use of flint, it was built of locally made bricks – the first time known since the departure of the Romans some 800 years before.

The growth of road transport ended passenger services on the Hadleigh branch in 1932, but wartime needs and those of local industry and agriculture kept the line open for goods until 1965.

Adnams' pubs: see Ipswich

The Mid-Suffolk Light Railway

One of the most prominent landmarks in Adnams' Country is the huge television mast at Mendlesham, a few miles north of Stowmarket. Built in 1959, it casts it shadow far and wide across this open rural part of Suffolk criss-crossed by winding country lanes and dotted with small villages. Yet the television mast was not the first great change to the landscape: that came in 1908 when the first passenger train ran on the Mid-Suffolk Light Railway (the MSLR).

Until then little had changed over the centuries; there were no large towns or any industrial developments. Agricultural products had to reach markets, but this was done the hard way. Cattle and sheep were herded along the roads and crops were moved by horse and cart to a rail-head, often very distant. It was only after the passing of a Light Railway Act in 1896 that there was any serious chance of a railway in central Suffolk; fewer regulations on signalling and safety and a 25mph speed limit opened up possibilities of country routes and rural stations.

The Mid-Suffolk Light Railway, locally known as the 'Middy', was planned to run from Haughley, the junction of the Great Eastern lines to Norwich and to Bury St Edmunds, to terminate over 27 miles to the east at Halesworth on the East Suffolk line. There, passengers

Hadleigh Station is now part of a residential estate.

Part of the Hadleigh-Bentley rail track is now a country walk.

would be able to transfer to the narrow gauge Southwold Railway or join the 'main' line to the east coast resorts, a convenient route for travellers from the Midlands. But the great local advantage would be a rail freight service from village stations and a public transport service for the scattered communities along land close to the MSLR line.

There were delays in starting the line and ambitious schemes for branches to the MSLR failed to materialise or were abandoned owing to shortage of finance. A problem arose in finding a feasible route into Halesworth and in due course several of the directors of the company lost large sums of money: as the records have it, 'The railway which ran from nowhere to the middle of a field'. Ultimately the last station was Laxfield although the line carried freight for a while to and from Laxfield Mills and Cratfield.

There were operating problems galore: water supplies for the locomotives were so unreliable that sometimes crews had to draw from a pond and there was no turntable at Laxfield. Shunting had to be done to pick up wagons at intermediate stations and crossing gates had to be operated by train crews, so the 19-mile route usually took at least 1½ hours for 'mixed' trains; passenger-only trains took over an hour. Some of the rural stations were a long way from village centres too.

The MSLR was said to be bankrupt before the first train ran, but those who knew it, remember it with affection; it had character. As elsewhere, road transport began to carry more and more goods traffic and by 1952 there were few passengers; the line was closed in July 1952.

Once the track had been lifted the station buildings were either removed or became dilapidated. Some were no more than huts; the farmer who went to his local station to pick up a hen hut he was expecting by rail took the station 'building' by mistake, or so it is said!

Having served mid-Suffolk for nearly fifty years the railway might have been forgotten altogether but for a group of enthusiasts who decided to keep the Middy's memory alive by recreating one of its stations: Brockford-Wetheringsett, to serve as a working museum.

Close to the A140 Norwich Road, a length of line could be laid there and used without disturbing residents. The local landowner was ready to lease the site and the track bed; work began

'Little Barford' at the MSLR's Museum at Brockford.

in 1991, incorporating the original Brockford cattle dock and extending it to create a 130-ft platform, with buildings from former MSLR stations.

The largest came from Mendlesham and housed the stationmaster's office and a store; between them is a waiting area. Another building came from Brockford itself, the station's former booking office.

When a steam train is operating at Brockford, tickets are sold at the entrance to the platform from a small booking office formerly at Wilby station. All the buildings have been painstakingly restored to their original appearance and condition.

While none of the Middy's rolling stock has survived, a locomotive similar to those that worked on the line has been acquired and is being restored. The museum also has 'Little Barford', which is in steam for special events at Brockford and hauls a passenger coach, a goods van and brake van identical with those used by the MSLR. There is a considerable length of track towards Aspall station, the ticket destination on 'Special Event' days. Restoration is ongoing particularly to other coach bodies, vacated now that a new refreshment room, shop and exhibition area have opened.

At the crossing gate, the end of the line at Brockford and a few yards from the road once crossed by MSLR trains there is a display of road vehicles in use when the line was working.

Directions:

Car parking is available on a field opposite to the museum's access road
Brown direction signs are posted from the A140
On reaching the Mendlesham mast take the sign for Park Green towards Wetheringsett

Museum opening hours:

Sundays in the summer
Wednesdays during August
For the MSLR programme of events ring 01449 766899.

Adnams' Pub:

Gladstone Arms   Combs Ford, Stowmarket   01449 612339

Snape

Wickham Market/Campsea Ashe station, way out in the country, was busier than might have been expected; it was not only the junction from Framlingham, but also handled freight services to and from Snape Maltings, now famous as a Concert Hall.

The 1½ mile Maltings spur had no passenger traffic and closed in 1960, having operated for some 100 years. There was a network of rail tracks at the Maltings and facilities for transferring freight to vessels at the wharf; the crops of local barley made the Maltings a profitable enterprise.

The line crossed the river at Snape where the bridge was somewhat fragile-looking: this limited the weight of the locomotive that could be used. In turn this made the climb from river level at the Maltings to the station at Wickham Market something of a challenge particularly in adverse conditions and trains were modest in size.

Adnams' pubs:

Crown Inn   Snape   01728 688324 (Accomm)
Golden Key   Snape   01728 688510

The Waveney Valley Railway

Even in its heyday, the Waveney Valley Railway was not one of East Anglia's most notable lines; to passengers unfamiliar with local geography the name 'Tivetshall to Beccles' might have been more meaningful. Its route was almost entirely in Norfolk; only short stretches at Bungay and Beccles were on the Suffolk side of the river.

From the very beginning the western end of the line, Tivetshall to Harleston, was the more important: this section was the first to open in 1855 and the last to close in 1966. Because the Waveney Valley line joined the main line from Ipswich to Norwich at Tivetshall, some Valley trains ran to and from Norwich Thorpe. Beccles, at the eastern end of the route and the junction on the East Suffolk line was less convenient and passengers had long waits for connections.

The final two sections of the line, connecting Harleston and Bungay then Bungay to Beccles were added in 1860 and 1863. The full 19½ miles of the branch were timetabled to take some fifty minutes, although that would vary according to the number of request stops at village stations such as Starston and Redenhall. These were closed in the early days of the line.

Harleston, now fortunately by-passed by the A134, is one of Norfolk's fine small market towns. The town's Georgian houses and the former Corn Exchange of 1849 are striking and the ancient Market Place, now partly built over, has a number of old houses round it. The tallest building is the Town Hall's Italianate tower.

The parish church is at Redenhall, over a mile away and is a fine example of flint flushwork so characteristic of the area. The great tower was begun in 1460 and stands prominently on high ground.

Harleston's thoroughfare is for northbound traffic only; look for Station Road on the left beyond the shops. The station building is handsome and well-preserved; today the headquarters of a construction company. To the left used to be a level crossing, a corn mill and maltings, today replaced by modern houses.

The spacious forecourt and large goods yard at the rear show this to have been a busy station; surprisingly the goods shed is still in use for stock needed to be kept under cover and secure. The layout of the former platforms can be readily seen today.

Starston is a pretty village 1½ miles west of Harleston. With your back to the church and look-ing across the river bridge up Railway Hill, the old station building stands on the brow of the hill (ten minutes up, five minutes down). The former railway track, now a public footpath at the rear of the house is unusually well preserved and is separated from the house by a traditional white fence.

East of Harleston a great deal of imagination is needed, as stations at Redenhall, Wortwell and Homersfield have gone. The line crossed the Beck at Homersfield, but only modern road bridges can be seen from the public footpath by the river: start at the Dove Inn.

At Earsham all there is to show is the old station house once the A143 had been built over the railway track. At Earsham village crossroads by the Dukes Head pub a 'no through road' leads to the former station. At the bottom of Station Road only a hedge and grass verge separate

Tivetshall, with the Waveney Valley line curving away east.

Harleston Station building on the Waveney Valley line is still in use as business premises.

An unusual garden gate on the Waveney Valley line near Pulham St Mary.

the building from traffic on the bypass. To the rear of the old station is a modern housing development with the appropriate name 'The Sidings'.

Bungay station disappeared along with the track when the bypass was built; only the tall former Maltings show where the line passed alongside towards Beccles.

At Ellingham there is an unusual feature: a road bridge over the track. Close to it a by-road leads to the old station building where there was once a level crossing. Much overgrown, the track can be easily identified.

Geldeston is an attractive yachting village; its station house and goods shed are in excellent order. Across the Ellingham Road from the goods yard is the track bed (well maintained and in private hands). Turn into The Street and see a fine example of a crinkle-crankle wall (Dutch style) round a private garden. Just beyond is Adnams' Wherry Inn.

Beccles Station is perhaps the saddest part of the whole line. This used to cross the river, go through level crossing gates near the bottom of Northgate and swing round past Beccles North Signal Box into Platform 1. This was a bay on the west side of the station with a goods yard next to it.

It hardly seems possible that when in full operation in addition to the main service to Liverpool street, the East Suffolk line continued north to Haddiscoe, St Olaves and Yarmouth Southtown (closed in 1959). A branch service (through trains too) went to Oulton Broad South and on to Lowestoft. Once threatened with closure, it was saved following fierce protests.

Beccles was once a busy station; there were more than fifty staff and an island platform as well as Platforms 1 and 2 for Waveney Valley and down trains from Ipswich.

Today Beccles is unstaffed and there is only a single track; nature has taken over the island platform and wherever weeds and undergrowth could flourish – they have. The sidings and goods yard next to Platform 1 serve as a storage site for building materials and a dump for rubble. Retired railwaymen must want to cry.

Adnams' pubs

| Butchers Arms | London Road, Beccles | 01502 712243 |
| Fleece Inn | St Mary's Street, Bungay | 01986 892192 |

A morning train from Tivetshall about to leave Bungay Station.

Ellingham Station House – its garden features the former platform.

Beccles Station with a Waveney Valley train at the bay platform.

Beccles Station, once a busy junction, is now a shadow of its former self.

All that is left of the Eye-Mellis line: the station master's house.

Bell Inn	Ferry Road, Walberswick	01502 723109 (Accomm)
Queens Head	Halesworth Road, Blyford	01502 478404 (Accomm)
Star Inn	Hall Road, Wenhaston	01502 478240

The Mellis and Eye Railway

This line opened – all three miles of it – in 1867. Eye's business interests feared the future when the route chosen for the Norwich main line passed through Diss to the west of Eye. Local pressure succeeded in having a branch built from a main line junction at Mellis, just south of Diss.

Passenger numbers were modest; a halt at Yaxley did little to raise them and freight consisted only of coal and agricultural produce. The passenger service ended in 1931 and in 1964 the line closed altogether.

The Yaxley to Eye stretch of the line has a few remaining traces to show its route: between the Cherry Tree pub and Yaxley Church is a road bridge where the station halt was set up. The line of the embankment can be seen here and there below it and beyond the A140 that passes close to Yaxley.

In Eye itself the Stationmaster's house has survived and has been incorporated as an office on an industrial estate; by its side the track bed leads through a wood into fields.

'Is that the Stationmaster's house?' I asked, 'If so, it could do with a makeover'. 'It's had one' was the reply. 'Must have been a long time ago' I suggested. My local contact agreed: 'Noah did it'.

Adnams' pubs:

| Cherry Tree | 74 London Road, Harleston | 01379 852345 |
| Cardinal's Hat | Thoroughfare, Harleston | 01379 853748 |

9

Suffolk Painters

John Constable

To have the countryside along the River Stour bordering Suffolk and Essex named 'Constable County' would be tribute enough, but for the *The Haywain* to be universally recognised – let alone many of Constable's other works – places him in a unique position in art history.

What is more, you can still explore Constable Country and recognise the scenes he painted. 'Here', you can say 'is where Constable set up his easel to paint Flatford Mill' and 'Here is the little bridge, a corner of Bridge Cottage and the entrance to the dry dock.' In the distance is the tower of Dedham Church; he called the painting *View on the Stour near Dedham.*

John's father owned Flatford Mill and several windmills round East Bergholt; one on East Bergholt common is in the distance in *Golding Constable's Kitchen Garden* at Christchurch Mansion, Ipswich.

As John was born at East Bergholt, that is where to begin an exploration of the countryside he loved – and loved to paint – more than any other. The village church has a stained glass window to his memory and his parents are buried close to the Bell Cage in the churchyard which houses the bells in the absence of a tower. The church was in the course of restoration in Wolsey's day and at his expense; it was never finished after his downfall, so it never had a new tower.

Downhill from the church is a large National Trust car park with access to the Bridge Cottage, and a little footbridge over the river. The Bridge Cottage serves as a Constable Centre for the trust and should be visited; upstream from the bridge is a view of Dedham Church and downstream are lock gates and Willy Lott's house, often in Constable's, paintings of Flatford. This scene, together with the view of the Mill buildings were the subject of his painting in 1817 now at the Tate Gallery.

From the north end of the bridge past The National Trust tea garden is the boat yard opened up by the trust: Constable's outdoor painting of this dated 1815 was called *Boat Building, Flatford Mill.* Beyond is the mill, now used as a countryside study centre; between the mill and Willy Lott's House is the mill pond and the wonderful view used by Constable for the *Haywain*. If you do not go to see this you will never forgive yourself.

Wherever you go here you will feel that John Constable has gone before; fragments of his countryside especially round Flatford Mill will seem familiar. A good preparation for a visit is the Suffolk Arts Trail published by Suffolk Tourism partnership and, of course an illustrated book of Constable's paintings.

Of the many Constable scenes to be explored, one had a boyhood memory for him. He used to walk some 1½ miles every day to Dedham, where he was a scholar at the grammar school, just opposite Dedham Church. A short distance below the village church at East Bergholt is narrow Fen Lane that leads across the fields to Dedham: John pictured a flock of sheep with a sheepdog and a little boy drinking from the stream. The church in the distance is not Dedham Church; John's inspiration was the thought of wind in the cornfield and stirring the trees. Walk down Fen Lane: the verge has changed and trees have grown, but you will feel part of *The Cornfield* of 1826 in the National Gallery, London.

Constable's paintings are on display at Christchurch Mansion, Ipswich (see p. 40) but if you know where to look, two of his works are on display in local churches where he was commissioned to paint altar pieces.

Fen Lane, John Constable's route to school at Dedham.

At Nayland is *Christ blessing the Bread and Wine*, which he painted for his aunt. Take A134 Sudbury-Colchester Road then B1087.

At Feering (originally at Manningtree) is *The Risen Christ*. For Feering take the A12 south-west of Colchester to Junction 24.

Adnams' pubs:

The Bull	The Street, Cavendish	01787 280245
Cock Inn	3 Callis Street, Clare	01787 277391
Red Lion	School Road, Great Wratting	01440 783237

Thomas Gainsborough and Gainsborough's House, Sudbury

A generation earlier than John Constable, Gainsborough was born in Sudbury in 1727, son of a cloth merchant; his statue is on the Market Place in front of St Peter's Church. Gainsborough House, his birthplace, now a museum and centre for the arts is at No. 46 Gainsborough Street.

After his death in 1788 Gainsborough was remembered with respect and great affection by his long-time rival Sir Joshua Reynolds who said at the Royal Academy 'This extraordinary man who was able to secure his effects by a kind of magic.'

As with John Constable, landscape was Gainsborough's first love; not actual scenes, although it was the Stour Valley that was his first inspiration. One of his earliest paintings became known as *Gainsborough's Forest*, or *Comard Wood* near Sudbury (in the National Gallery, London). It was for mood and effect that Gainsborough used landscape: sunsets, sunlight through trees and reflections in water.

His training began at the age of thirteen when he went to London to work in the studio of Hubert Gravelot, an illustrator and designer. He was introduced to Hogarth, but his connections did not bring success when he opened his own London studio and he returned to

Gainsborough's House, Sudbury, now a gallery and art centre.

Sudbury in 1748, by now married to the beautiful Margaret Burr who had a useful annuity from the Duke of Beaufort.

One of his Sudbury paintings was of Mr and Mrs Andrews, a young married couple pictured against the family estate of Auberies just outside Sudbury (in the National Gallery, London). Painted against an ancient oak tree, the attractive Mrs Andrews shows up beautifully, with blue highlights in her dress sculpted by Gainsborough's brushwork. It was not long before he realised that to attract commissions they would have to move to Ipswich, the county town, which they did in 1752.

He entered Ipswich's social life, obtaining commissions to paint owners of local estates, such as William Wollaston of Finborough Hall (in Christchurch Mansion, Ipswich). People in public life were also painted: the Revd Richard Canning and Mrs Samuel Kilderbee (both in Christchurch Mansion, Ipswich).

One of his closest friends at Ipswich was Philip Thicknesse, Governor of Landguard Fort near Felixstowe. He took the credit for persuading Gainsborough to move to Bath where he established his reputation for painting lovely ladies.

In his lifetime Gainsborough painted some 800 portraits, 200 landscapes and about twenty 'Fancy' pictures (sentimental scenes that took his fancy). The National Gallery in London has a fine collection that includes great examples of his work, but it was not until 1961 that Gainsborough's House in Sudbury was acquired and officially opened as a 'fitting monument to Thomas Gainsborough'.

The collection at Sudbury has been supplemented by loans from the Arts Council, other galleries and from private owners. Appeals were launched to finance repairs and redecoration and to provide better lighting and hanging facilities.

Gradually there was acceptance of the importance of Gainsborough's House and increased support came from Suffolk County Council, Babergh District Council, Sudbury Town Council and Friends of Gainsborough's House.

To acquire the property many individuals worked to raise funds or made donations themselves; the largest single donor was Sir Alfred Munnings, from Castle House, Dedham.

Castle House, Dedham, once the home of Sir Alfred Munnings.

The Gainsborough House Society was formed in 1958 and its centenary was marked in 2008 by *Gainsborough's House: a Golden Celebration*.

Supported by the Heritage Lottery Fund the House had a major refurbishment in 2005–2006. Apart from an increase in the Gallery space and a redecoration and repair of the whole house, a lift was installed and a Study Gallery fitted out; improvements to the lighting system have also been made.

As a fine example of Gainsborough's brilliant use of light look for *Wooded Landscape* which he portrayed at sunset with reflections in a pool. The Sudbury collection has examples of Gainsborough's work from the whole of his career; acquisitions have included *Portrait of a Boy* and more recently John Vere and Mary Vere painted in about 1753. On permanent loan are *Countess Dartmouth* and *Portrait of Harriet, Viscountess Tracy*; look at the lace on her gown!

Gainsborough's assistant, his nephew Gainsborough Dupont, was a talented painter and examples of his work are to be seen, too.

An Education Centre has been established on the first floor and a print workshop, opened in 1970, is located next to the Main Entrance in Weavers' Lane.

To study Gainsborough's work more fully, the following works are recommended:

National Gallery of Scotland:

The Hon. Mrs Graham

National Gallery London:
Cornard Wood
Mr & Mrs Andrews
Gainsborough's daughters
The Watering Place
Mrs Sarah Siddons
The Morning Walk
The Market Cart

Dedham Church was a favourite subject of both Munnings and Constable.

Tate Gallery London
Giovanna Baccelli
Kenwood
Mary, Countess Howe

Gainsborough's House Opening Hours:

Monday to Saturday 10 a.m. to 5 p.m.
Tuesdays from 1 p.m. to 5 p.m. (free)

Directions:

From Sudbury Market Hill walk to the corner of Gainsborough St. Turn right into Weaver's Lane.

Adnams' pubs:

The Bull	The Street, Cavendish	01787 280245
Cock Inn	3 Callis Street, Clare	01787 277391
Red Lion	School Road, Great Wratting	01440 783237

Sir Alfred Munnings and Castle House, Dedham

Castle House was Munnings' home and studio for the last forty years of his life. Dedham village church with its fine tower often painted by John Constable should be visited when going to Castle House. The church has a beautiful carved pew presented by the people of Dedham, USA as part of the church's restoration.

Munnings loved to include Dedham church tower, too, in his local paintings. He was born in Suffolk at Mendham, in the Waveney Valley; his father was a miller as was John Constable's.

In spite of losing the sight of one eye at the age of twenty when caught by a briar, his great success as a painter is all the more remarkable. His first job was as a poster artist in Norwich, but his studies at the Norwich School of Art quickly led to a painting being accepted by the Royal Academy at the early age of nineteen.

He travelled and painted abroad as well as in this country, but because of the partial loss of his sight was unable to serve in the First World War; he was sent to join the Canadian Cavalry Brigade in 1918 as an official war artist.

Munning's paintings in France led to several private commissions and his reputation became established as the greatest horse painter since the time of George Stubbs. He was elected president of the Royal Academy in 1944 and was honoured in that year; on his death in 1959 his pictures and estate were left to the nation. His widow Lady Munnings worked to ensure this and to the setting up of Castle House as an Art Museum now administered by the Castle House Trust.

A visit to Castle House, a blend of Tudor and Georgian styles, including his studio, is exciting in itself, apart from the fine collection of Munning's paintings on display. Although he did not paint a thoroughbred until 1919, he believed that horses were his destiny and he had a particular ability to portray both rider and horse. He loved the racing scene: at Castle House is one of his best paintings *Study of a Start at Newmarket, 1951*.

An early 'domestic' painting of 1908, 'The Path to the Orchard' shows his pony Augereau being led along the riverbank at Mendham and *My wife, my Horse and Myself* is lovingly painted against the back of the house.

Munnings was a much more versatile painter than is often thought: he enjoyed both the East Anglian countryside and its people, showing great understanding and fluency. Look for *Susan at the Fair*, full of colour and movement, *Portrait of Nelly Gray*, a character study in red and *Tagg's Island*, a party group in the style of Hogarth's nineteenth-century conversation piece.

All of those paintings are in the Munnings' Collection at Castle House, but there are many more further afield such as *Sunny June* and *Horse Sale* at the Castle Museum, Norwich. *Travellers* at Christchurch, Mansion, Ipswich, shows ponies and a rider in the Waveney Valley in Suffolk.

For background material *A.J. Munnings* by Stanley Booth (Sothebys) and, of course, *The Munnings Collection*, the guide from Castle House are valuable.

I particularly like the story of Munnings' *Inspiration:* the skewbald pony he bought in a weak moment as part of a 'deal' from a dealer in Bungay who arrived to deliver a second hand bureau to his home. Munnnings said it would bring him luck and it did: he painted *Ponies at the Fair* and put the new pony in the foreground. It drew great critical acclaim especially for showing Munnings' love of the landscape and sold well.

Opening Times for Castle House:

Sundays, Wednesdays and Bank Holiday Mondays
Thursdays and Saturdays in August 2 p.m. to 5. p.m.
Tel. 01206 322127
There is a free car park; if walking, the house is a pleasurable
¾ mile from the village, on the corner of East Lane, Castle Hill.

Adnams' pubs:

Bull	The Street, Cavendish	01787 280245
Cock Inn	3 Callis Street, Clare	01787 277391
Red Lion	School Road, Great Wratting	01440 783237

Adnams' Pubs

Anchor Inn	The Street, Walberswick	01502 722112 (Accomm)
Angel Hotel	The Thoroughfare, Halesworth	01986 873365 (Accomm)
Bell Inn	Ferry Road, Walberswick	01502 723109 (Accomm)
Bell Inn	The Green, Middleton	01728 648286
Black Tiles	Black Tiles Lane, Martlesham	01473 624038
Blyth Hotel	Station Road, Southwold	01502 722632 (Accomm)
Bull Inn	The Street, Cavendish, Sudbury	01787 280245
Butchers Arms	London Road, Beccles	01502 712243
Cardinal's Hat	Thoroughfare, Harleston	01379 85374
Castle Inn	Castle Street, Cambridge	01223 353194
Cherry Tree	73 Cumberland Street, Woodbridge	01394 382513 (Accomm)
Cherry Tree	74 London Road, Harleston	01379 852345
Cock Inn	3 Callis Street, Clare	01787 277391
County	29 St Helens Street, Ipswich	01473 255153
Cross Keys	Crabbe Street, Aldeburgh	01728 452637 (Accomm)
Crown Inn	Bridge Road, Snape	01728 688324 (Accomm)
Duke of York	Woodbridge Road, Ipswich	01473 257115
Eel's Foot Inn	Leiston Road, Eastbridge	01728 830154
Engineers Arms	7 Main Street, Leiston	01728 830660
Five Bells	Southwold Road, Wrentham	01502 675249 (Accomm)
Fleece Inn	St Mary's Street, Bungay	01986 892192
Gladstone Arms	Combs Ford, Stowmarket	01449 612339
Golden Key	Priory Road, Snape	01728 688510 (Accomm)
Greyhound	9 Henley Road, Ipswich	01473 252862
Half Moon	303 High Street, Walton	01394 216009
Harbour Inn	Blackshore, Southwold	01502 722381
Horse & Groom	London Road, Wrentham	01502 675279
Jolly Sailor	Quay Street, Orford	01394 450243
King's Head	Front Street, Orford	01394 450271 (Accomm)
Kings Head	High Street, Southwold	01502 724517 (Accomm)
Kings Head	17 Market Hill, Woodbridge	01394 387750
Lord Nelson Inn	East Street, Southwold	01502 722079
Lord Nelson	Fore Street, Ipswich	01473 254072
Mill Inn	Market Cross, Aldeburgh	01728 452563
Oyster Inn	Woodbridge Road, Butley	01394 450790
Prince Consort	11 Nelson Road, Great Yarmouth	01493 843268
Queen's Head	Blyford, Halesworth	01502 478404 (Accomm)
Queen's Head	The Street, Bramfield	01986 784214
Queen's Head	The Street, Long Stratton	01508 530164
Railway Inn	Leiston Road, Aldeburgh	01728 453864
Railway Inn	9 Station Road, Framlingham	01728 723693
Randolph Hotel	41 Wangford Road, Reydon	01502 723603 (Accomm)
Red Lion	School Road, Great Wratting	01440 783237
Sole Bay Inn	East Green, Southwold	01502 723736
Star Inn	Hall Road, Wenhaston	01502 478240
Swan Hotel	Market Place, Southwold	01502 722186 (Accomm)
Wherry Inn	7 The Street, Geldeston, Beccles	01508 518371
White Hart	High Street, Aldeburgh	01728 453205
White Hart	London Road, Blythburgh	01502 478217 (Accomm)
White Hart	The Thoroughfare, Halesworth	01986 873386
White Horse	Darsham Road, Westleton	01728 648222 (Accomm)

Acknowledgements

Nothing prepared me for so generous a response from people who live and work in Adnams Country. My search for information and illustrations became theirs, my problems theirs too; a wildly impossible idea became a challenge to be fulfilled immediately. Miracles, I felt might have taken a little longer.

In thanking them all, I ask forgiveness for any names omitted below. Any errors or omissions are my responsibility entirely.

I wish everyone tempted to visit (or revisit) places illustrated in this book an enjoyable and eventful journey in 'selig' Suffolk:

Jonathan Adnams, executive chairman, Adnams PLC; Emma Hibbert, corporate affairs manager, Adnams PLC; Dr I.R.L.T Beaumont, Otley Hall; Helga Brandt, Theatre Royal, Bury St Edmunds; R.M. Casserley (Casserley Collection); Colin Challis, Lowestoft Porcelain; Geoffrey Crabb, Southwold Railway Trust; The Hon. Hugh Crossley, Somerleyton Hall; His Grace the Duke of Grafton, Euston Hall; Linda Campbell, Euston Hall; Alex Hall, National Stud, Newmarket; Jane Hart, Bawdsey Manor; Laura Kerr, Easton Farm Park; John Marsh, Suffolk Punch Trust; Neil and Gill Mason, Sibton White Horse; Peter Parker, chairman, Lowestoft & East Suffolk Maritime Society; Diane Perkins, Gainsborough's House, Sudbury; Nick Read, Harleston; Chris Reeve, Bungay Museum; Diane Roe, Sir Alfred Munnings Art Museum; Julia Vinson, Ickworth; Jeremy Watson, Henry Watson's Potteries, Wattisfield.

Valuable help of all kinds was offered by the Suffolk Development Agency, tourist information centres and museums as follows:

Brandon, Colchester and Ipswich Museums Service; Flixton (Norfolk & Suffolk Aviation Museum); Lowestoft (Broad House Museum, Oulton Broad); Lowestoft (Carlton Colville East Anglia Transport Museum); Mid-Suffolk Light Railway Museum (Wetheringsett-cum-Brockford); Stowmarket Museum of East Anglian Life (MEAL);

Ipswich Borough Council; Ipswich Port Authority; Christchurch Mansion; the Unitarian Meeting House; Orwell River Cruises at Ipswich; The Royal Society for the Protection of Birds: Minsmere and Havergate Island; Walpole Old Chapel.

To good friends Barry and Laura, who transformed my inadequate typescript into material ready for the printer I am more grateful than I can say. Their advice was invaluable.

Finally, to my editors Michelle Tilling and Nicola Guy at The History Press, my heartfelt thanks; their optimism and reassurance always brought hope when it was most needed. Under their guidance the book and the author could not have been in better hands.

Peter Thomas
April 2009